Performance Coaching for Complex Projects

For Julie, in recognition of her unwavering confidence that I could complete this project.

Performance Coaching for Complex Projects

Influencing Behaviour and Enabling Change

TONY LLEWELLYN

LONDON AND NEW YORK

First published 2015 by Gower Publishing

2 Park Square, Milton Park, Abingdon, Oxon, OX14 4RN
605 Third Avenue, New York, NY 10017

Routledge is an imprint of the Taylor & Francis Group, an informa business

First issued in paperback 2020

British Library Cataloguing in Publication Data
A catalogue record for this book is available from the British Library.

Library of Congress Cataloging-in-Publication Data
Llewellyn, Tony (Executive coach)
Performance coaching for complex projects : influencing behaviour and enabling change / by Tony Llewellyn.
pages cm. – (Advances in project management)
Includes bibliographical references and index.
ISBN 978-1-4724-6180-3 (hardback) – ISBN 978-1-4724-6181-0 (ebook) – ISBN 978-1-4724-6182-7 (epub)
1. Teams in the workplace. 2. Employees – Coaching of. I. Title.

HD66.L57 2015
658.3'124–dc23

2015020656

ISBN 13: 978-1-4724-6180-3 (hbk)
ISBN 13: 978-0-367-73758-0 (pbk)

Contents

List of Figures

List of Tables

Preface

Commissioning a major project is a journey into unchartered territory. The project starts with an idea in someone's head, and ends with an outcome that will be used in some way or other, to improve the lives of human beings. The journey begins with the assembly of the different specialists until a group is formed that calls itself a team. This group will travel together in one form or another for the duration of the project, losing some members along the way and picking up others. Sometimes this is a journey of exciting exploration as the group manages to work together to overcome obstacles and other misfortunes. More often than not, it is a struggle through rough and unexpected terrain, taking longer and costing more to reach the final destination.

There are many factors that influence whether the project will find a rough or a smooth passage and so it is difficult to create a route map setting out the optimum path. There is, however, sufficient research to conclude that one of the key determinants of project success is the extent to which the members of the group focus not only on their own technical contribution, but also engage with the other members to find solutions that help the project reach completion. That is when they transform from being a group to a real team.

Any group of people who are collected together will seek out a leader. On major projects, the leader is more often than not carrying out the role of the project manager (PM). As a professional discipline, the role of the PM is still developing, but the formal training that most PMs receive is focused on technical proficiency. Many people, including PMs themselves, criticise the profession for its concentration on task completion. In the past, there has been limited attention paid to the management of the human interaction. This book works around a central notion that the common transactional mindsets and methodologies that may have worked on complicated projects will not produce the required result when applied to more complex undertakings. As we discuss in Chapter 1, complexity requires a different approach to managing the most expensive and underused resource on any project – the people.

My proposition is that the PM or team leader should coach the team as part of their role. The concept of coaching a team engaged on a large project is still quite novel. Executive coaching of individuals has only been established as a mainstream commercial activity for the last 15 years. The successful growth of the coaching industry has been based on the recognition that individuals sometimes need help to think through their problems and dilemmas. Team coaching is more ambitious, in that one of the primary roles of the team coach is to help the team work together to think through their issues and then collectively implement the solution.

The team therefore needs to have a collective approach to the ways in which they engage with each other. The evidence from many different research studies indicates that the few teams who get it right, usually succeed. On the other hand, virtually everyone who has worked on a major capital project has first hand experience of what happens when human behaviour is no longer aligned to the project goals.

The problem is that people are messy. Our personalities and motivations are often not immediately obvious. Every new project offers the prospect that the members of the group may or may not gel. Once we have experienced working in a good team we recognise that it is exciting and professionally satisfying. We also know that a bad team experience can drain our energy and become highly stressful. And yet most project leaders still tend to leave the teamwork aspect of a project to chance. There is often a flawed assumption that, provided everybody on the team does their job, the project outcome will be fine. This assumption often turns out to be incorrect and the team experience disappoints and frustrates.

My arguments are therefore structured around the need to understand the behaviours of the team, both as individuals and as a group. Managing complexity requires greater use of influence and less reliance on coercion. Learning how to recognise the clues that reveal personal preferences, character traits and motivations will allow you to communicate in a way that recognises how different team members see the world. This requires working at a different pace, where time invested early in the project cycle will enable faster progress later on. This calls for a leap of faith.

A common caricature of a PM is someone who has a preference for action over debate, putting a low priority on the need to recognise personal emotions in the context of task completion. If you are a PM, there is a chance that you are already sceptical about the subject of behavioural change. Your instinct may be telling you to close this book now and get on with something useful! The challenge remains that if you want to improve your ability to manage performance on complex projects, then a basic understanding as to what motivates and engages other people is essential.

This book works through the various opportunities and challenges that groups of specialists face as they go about the business of creating something that did not previously exist. It looks at the various factors that will decide where a collection of professionals sits on the continuum between a high-performing team at one end of the spectrum and the dysfunctional and ineffective group at the other. More importantly, it provides some ideas and processes that team leaders can use to coach the project team so that, even if it is not moving up the performance scale, the group is at least holding ground and avoiding the descent into dysfunction and litigation.

Structure

The book is structured in two parts. Part I looks at the challenges of complexity and makes the case for the development of a new skill set to cope with the challenges of the twenty-first century. The underlying theme is to make a shift from a transactional directive mindset to a transformational coaching philosophy. The next chapter considers some of the theory around team coaching as it can be applied to large projects. Chapter 3 provides a basic introduction to the psychological factors that influence team behaviour. In Part II, I introduce a model of project team coaching to provide a structure around which to build your coaching practice. Chapters 4, 5 and 6 set out a range of processes and methodologies that have been shown to be effective in improving team performance. The book closes with a look at your personal learning, and anticipates how complexity is likely to shape the way organisations are likely to approach projects over the next 20 or so years.

Stories

Much of the content of the book is derived from my research into the published thinking of experts in the fields of team performance, group psychology, team coaching and advanced project management practices. It has also been shaped by the stories that I have collected as I interviewed people who have spent much of their working lives on major projects. When I first thought about writing this book, I wanted to understand how the theories put forward by the experts played out in real life. I therefore sought out men and women who had experience of delivering complex projects for a range of public and private organisations. My initial objective was to explore their views on management technique and process, but I found that the greatest degree of insight came from their stories.

Stories are not scientific, in so far as they rely on unreliable memories which distort the actual events to make sense of an outcome, or to emphasise a point. They are nevertheless the best mechanisms for humans to reflect on the past and learn from it. I listened to many tales of successes achieved against the odds, and failure that derived from discarded opportunity. These stories have helped me find a series of threads that appear to run through many different types of project. I hope that by pulling together the various strands of the experiences of others, you can find a degree of resonance with your own stories that will enable you to also learn from them.

My objective in writing this book has been to write something that is academically credible but more importantly is also of practical use. I have picked out material from a wide range of sources. The books and articles that are referenced throughout have been assembled to develop a coherent argument for change. I would particularly like to acknowledge the works of David Clutterbuck and Peter Hawkins upon whom I have often relied to guide the emergence of my thinking as to how coaching might apply to teams working on complex projects.

Real Life

One of the problems with books such as this one is that they are written in the quiet space of the writer's study, where the author can reflect on what should happen when everybody behaves in a calm and rational manner. They are not written in the middle of a hectic day when budgets are stretched, the technology is erratic and your inbox is growing. Real life has a habit of getting in the way of a good theory. It is often easy for the reader to find a gap between the concepts and ideas expressed in a book and their own day-to-day experience. This book should not necessarily therefore be read as a manual on how to manage and coach project teams. My intention is to provide you with an alternative perspective based on the research of others and the stories that I have collected. Where I thought it was useful, I have included a number of ideas and suggestions as to how you might develop your own working practices. Ultimately, however, it is for you to take these ideas and decide for yourself how they might apply to your own world.

Making Contact

There have been times when reading through the works of others that I had wanted to make contact with the author, either to ask a question or sometimes simply to thank them for inspiring me to continue to write. Some are easier to find than others. I see myself on a learning journey that will continue into the future. Writing this book is just another step along the way. I am therefore pleased to share the stories and ideas that I will continue to collect. If you want to contact me, you can find me through the website www.projectteamcoaching.com or you can email me at tony@thefairlightproject.com.

Tony Llewellyn

The Storytellers

I would like to thank the following people for giving up their time to tell me their stories:

Richard Baldwin

Laurence Barea

Peter Barker

Phil Brittan

Graham Caldwell

Alastair Collins

Marie Dariel

Tim Fitch

Nick Fleming

Jim French

Lee Griffin

David Hancock

Paul Harris

Jez Haskins

John Hicks

Despina Katsikakis

Tim Knee Robinson

Harpy Lally

Nick Leggett

John Lewis

David Long

Christian Male

Matt Nicholson

Cathy O'Driscoll

Mike Parker

Scott Price

Charles Roe

Nick Schumann

Charlotte Semp

Kevin Sims

Rob Smith

Anita Suji

Michael Tost

Adam Trigg

Paul Wheeler

Note: In the interests of confidentiality not all of the names match the stories described in the book.

PART I

A New Skill Set for the Twenty-first Century

Chapter 1

The Challenge of Managing Complexity

This book is about those components of teamwork that are not set out in a legal document or performance specification. It is about how, as project manager (PM) and project leader, you tap into the only resource that can make complex projects work – human ingenuity.

Graham is a PM who specialises in projects in the rail industry. In 2009 he led a team delivering part of a major project to upgrade the rail link between Edinburgh and Bathgate. Rail work is complex. It requires several major contracting organisations to work together, providing civil engineering, rail construction, signalling and other technical operations. The complexity comes from the need to work in a live environment. This means that at the end of every shift, the team need to leave the site in a state that is safe for trains to run through it. It needs to be 100 per cent safe, not just reasonably safe. The scope for miscommunication and error is particularly high as there are so many interfaces to tie up between the different contractors. This project stands out in Graham's memory as a great example of collaborative working. The timetable was tight and the team were constantly fighting the elements to stay on programme. Given the unpredictable Scottish weather, the fact that the project was delivered only one month behind schedule was quite remarkable.

I asked Graham what made this contract work when so many other infrastructure projects run substantially over time and over budget. He was able to identify some key environmental factors such as a well-prepared brief and a knowledgeable client. The critical distinction however was the project environment, where each organisation worked together with a single focus, even though there was no formal contract between them. The project worked because everyone appeared to understand that if one of the contractors failed, so did everybody else.

Teamwork

What comes to mind when you first think of the phrase 'teamwork'? To some, it means a group of people working efficiently and effectively to complete a task. To others it creates an image of too much talking and not enough action. Your mental picture will be influenced by your experiences and your personal motivations. For the reasons discussed later in the book, many of our team experiences are negative. It is therefore surprising that, as a rule, people still have a high degree of faith in the potential of teams. Psychologists and social historians believe that our attraction to teams is hardwired into our brains and goes back to our prehistoric origins, where the ability to hunt for food in groups was the key to survival. In the modern age, we continue to create teams on a regular basis. When there is a big problem to solve, the instinct is to assemble a set of individuals with complementary skills who can work together. The problem is that quite often they don't.

People are complicated. Our psychological motivations are shaped by many different factors, some genetic, others learned. Childhood influences become overlaid by social norms so that by the time we reach adulthood, most of us have worked out how to establish and maintain social and professional relationships, at least at a superficial level. So whilst we can appear to make good social connections with the other members of a new group, there is a lot of 'stuff' going on underneath the surface. We know from experience that most people will, over time, reveal a series of behaviours that will impact the effectiveness of the group.

Studies of people working in groups consistently confirm that each individual's behaviours can be strongly influenced, for better or for worse, by other members of the group. The individual with the most influence will typically be the group leader. On large projects, the leader will invariably be undertaking the role, in whole or in part, of the 'project manager'. As the leader, you are the one who is responsible for creating and maintaining the dynamics of a successful team. Of course, the PM role is multifaceted. You may have the role of client representative, programme co-ordinator, or quite literally the manager of the project. Whatever the title, if you are the one person that the other team members turn to when there is a question for which they do not know the answer, then you are the primary influencer.

Is this what you signed up for when you decided to become a PM? Probably not. Most PMs come into the role from some other trade or professional discipline. You got the job because you were good at organising. No one said anything about being good at 'influence'. I believe however, that as projects become increasingly complex, this is the one skill that will distinguish good PMs from the rest of the pack. The underlying theme of this book is how, as the leader of the team, you make a shift in your own behavioural strategy, and learn when to change from the tactics of coercion to those of influence.

The Project Management Role is Evolving

The shift from organiser to influencer is probably not a choice. The world is changing, presenting both threats and opportunities, and if you are to remain successful in this career, it is probably a good idea to consider what is happening outside of your immediate environment. The forces of change are more complicated than they used to be.

THE WORLD IS CHANGING

We increasingly work in a global economy. Wherever your project is based, it will be affected by whatever is happening elsewhere around the world. Forecasters predict shorter economic cycles and less stable political environments. Organisational hierarchies are changing, causing more frequent disruption to high-level decision making. Similarly, environmental challenges and energy scarcity will continue to create continuous shifts in economic and social behaviour. The result is likely to be increased pressure to deliver project outcomes more quickly.

PROJECTS ARE CHANGING

The population in many parts of the world are moving into urban centres. This shift is creating a need for more accommodation as well as all the infrastructure and services that are required to support increased population density. We are likely to see an increasing growth in 'smart city' technology, where utilities, transport infrastructure and public services are all linked to create an efficient and competitive environment. Many projects will have an increase in engineering and technology components, requiring greater interaction between technical specialists and multiple stakeholders. Big projects will also create a need for larger 'distributed' teams, working from different locations, often in different countries.

THE DEMAND FOR PM SKILLS IS CHANGING

Basic project management services are going to become increasingly commoditised. Professions that rely on discrete knowledge are already finding that someone, somewhere, is prepared to do that work for a lower fee. It is no longer a strategy to rely on technical knowledge to maintain competitive advantage. The basic information upon which knowledge workers have traditionally relied is now readily available for anyone who cares to search for it. Less obvious, but probably more significant, is the need to recognise that advances in data analysis software will mean that significant chunks of knowledge-based activity will eventually be automated. Professions that rely primarily on their awareness of how to navigate around the rules are going to struggle. It is therefore quite possible that the processing component of the traditional project management service of the future may either be outsourced or automated. The outlook for the PM might therefore appear a little bleak. On a more positive note, for the foreseeable future, at least, the one thing that digital technology will not be able to replace is the management of the successful interactions between human beings.

Collaborative Working

As projects grow in size and complexity, there will be an increased need for organisations to work collaboratively. The size of global markets make the prize for success much greater, but the scale of ambition will often exceed the capability and capacity of organisations to deliver a project if they work alone. We are therefore likely to see an increase in demand for projects based on partnering and collaborative ventures, both as a way of maximising resource and reducing risk.

Collaborative teamwork requires a shift in mindset that needs to move beyond transactional thinking. The word collaboration means different things to different people, but from a project perspective I like the following definition. 'Collaboration is a reciprocal process in which two or more individuals or organisations work together. It assumes that participants have common objectives. In general, they seek more benefits, by forming a collaborative relationship in which they are required to share resources and knowledge, than by working alone' (Son and Rojas, 2011).

Collaboration therefore also involves an element of risk and so requires the team to develop a high degree of interpersonal trust. It is about giving something up in anticipation of a future benefit that is not yet defined as a contractual obligation. It is almost impossible to work collaboratively where either, or both, of the parties is holding back to see who is the first one to expose themselves to the risk of non-reciprocation.

The problem with collaboration is that it is easy to talk about, but more difficult to implement. Joint ventures are often dreamt up over the boardroom table by senior executives who are can see the potential synergies of two organisations applying their complementary skills to achieve a common goal. Once the headline terms of the joint venture are agreed, then quite frequently the responsibility for implementation is dropped down to a number of managers who are tasked with getting on with the job. The problem in many joint ventures is that their middle managers are used to working in a transactional manner, so any sense of common goals tends to be lost 'in translation'.

Some people have a natural predisposition to collaborate. They have a strong internal belief in the power of teams and have learned to quickly build trusting relationships. More often, however, those tasked with the implementation of a joint venture have a transactional mindset which places limited value on interpersonal skills and is more concerned with risk. More time is spent trying to tie down contractual obligations and less time is invested in building relationships. By the time that the project gets underway, the prospect of finding potential synergies has been lost.

The Advanced PM

This book is published under a series title of Advances in Project Management. The series is a response to the growing recognition that the PM skill set needs to evolve to accommodate their changing role. Michael Cavanagh (2012) makes the case that PMs need to move on from the traditional toolkit of systems such as Earned Value Management, PRINCE2 and other PM processes. He is keen to emphasise that these tools are still valuable but, in themselves, they are not going to be sufficient to solve the challenges that come with complex projects. Cavanagh identifies a number of additional skills that will help the PM move to the next level or Second Order. Those include processes such as *systemic thinking, outcome management, experiential learning* and *appropriate contracting*. I see tremendous value in each of these propositions, but would add another fundamental capability, which is to learn the *interpersonal* skills that are required to lead a team through a complex environment.

The curriculum for most project management training includes a notional element of team development, but my observation is that it is given a low priority. For example, the competency framework used by the Royal Institution of Chartered Surveyors (RICS) (2015) requires a PM seeking accreditation to demonstrate an awareness of 'different styles of leadership, and of different motivation theories'. It also asks for an 'understanding of the ingredients that are necessary to create high performing teams'. Yet when I talk to colleagues who have the RICS qualification, they look slightly puzzled when I ask them where they found their source information to develop this awareness. The reality is that such people-oriented skills are given a low priority in most forms of project management training.

This is not surprising since the people who design the training competency frameworks can only do so within the context of their own experience. For most young professionals, the learning process is structured around a progression from simple contracts to larger more complicated projects. There is, quite rightly, a strong emphasis on building the technical foundations upon which other skills can be built. The problem, as I perceive it, is that people-oriented skills are not yet regarded as a critically important component of the PM skill set. They are an optional extension to the development programme. My view is that, in the future, skills such as leadership, communication and relationship management are going to be more prominent in the development of a qualified PM. In reading this book, you are simply giving yourself a chance to get ahead of the curve.

Escaping the Transactional Mindset

Making the transition from organiser to influencer requires a fundamental adjustment in the way that you perceive your role when a project moves from *complicated* to *complex*. The big question is whether you are you able to recognise the extent to which your thinking is governed by a transactional mindset?

We live in a society where a lot of our day-to-day activity is conducted on a transactional basis. To give an example, I might pay you a sum of money to do the things that are necessary to achieve the specific outcome that I am looking for. The more that I understand what it is you do, the more comfortable I am in seeking an alternative price for the service you offer. We contract with each other, you deliver the service and I write you a cheque. This is lovely and simple. There is limited need to build any sort of relationship if I choose not to, and I have no further obligation to you once the project has been completed. This transactional process requires one key element to work efficiently. We both need a *high level of certainty* as to what is required. I need to know that you can do what I need to be done, and you need to understand clearly what I want doing.

If all business could be done on this basis, commercial life would be much less stressful. In practice, of course, it is not, and yet there is an underlying tendency in all businesses to try to reduce commercial interactions to the lowest common denominator of the simple transaction. In the rush to develop efficient processes and methodologies, we have often removed context from the equation. The inexperienced PM can follow the rulebook, and 'join up the dots', but will often struggle to recognise the clues and signals that offer solutions before they become problems. Many managers never learn how to develop the interpersonal skills that are required to handle arrangements that contain a level of ambiguity or uncertainty.

The Conspiracy of Optimism

As discussed later in this chapter, complexity arises when there are too many unknown variables affecting the project. How can you enter into a transactional relationship with a client/stakeholder when he does not yet know exactly what he wants, and you don't know exactly how to provide it? Cavanagh (2012) makes reference to the 'Conspiracy of Optimism' where clients, delivery agents and suppliers press on with a project on a transactional basis. They know that this approach is unlikely to achieve the performance criteria needed to achieve the desired outcome. They just hope that it all turns out for the best. Each of them is aware that there are so many uncertainties in the project that they should not rationally enter into any form of guarantee in terms of price or delivery date.

I see the transactional mindset as being the greatest barrier to the progression of understanding as to how teams can operate at a higher level of performance. The challenge is not simply a matter of rationally examining what worked or did not work in the past. Transactional thinking offers the illusion of security. Sticking to organisational processes that are familiar obviates the need to take any personal risk in decision making. I have frequently encountered decision makers who will revert to transactional process, even when presented with evidence that this strategy failed to produce the desired result in the past. The transactional mindset tends towards a belief that past failures can be attributed to personal error, and that everything will be different on the next project. The *conspiracy of optimism* creeps in, as each member of the supply team rejects those nagging thoughts that remind us that transactional thinking didn't work very well last time, or even the time before that. Our desire is simply for the project to progress. If you doubt the strength of the transactional mindset, it is worth considering the way that it often overrides the more logical question which is, 'Are we sure we are going to make a profit from our involvement with this project?'

Large projects require an expensive step into the unknown. At a superficial level, it is quite rational to try and use transactional processes to create a framework around which certainty can develop. A problem starts when the pressure of urgency means that projects move into implementation before the framework has developed to a level where transactional arrangements might be effective. If you rush to get a project started before you have decided exactly what you need, then you're going to have difficulty forcing your suppliers to work to fixed contractual arrangements. A transactional mindset only really works when you have the time to make detailed plans, but then what do you do when the plans have to change?

The alternative is to adopt a collaborative mindset, where the rules of engagement between the project sponsor, the team leader and the team participants work on a much more personal basis. If you look beneath the surface of any business that can demonstrate long-term success, you will find that they are part of a series of relatively stable supply chains, where interpersonal relationships are strong and business exchanges work on a collaborative basis. Documentation is used to instigate commercial contracts, but the efficiency of delivery relies on communication between individuals who understand what needs to be achieved and will make their own adjustments where necessary without having to resort to a claim using the formal documentation.

The challenge for a PM tasked with the leadership of a complex project is first of all to make your own adjustment from a transactional mindset to a collaborative perspective. Critically, you then need to be able to influence both your sponsor and your team to achieve the same paradigm shift. My mission in writing this book is to give you some tools that will help your articulate your message.

Complex versus Complicated

At the core of my thinking on collaborative working is the challenge of complexity. It is a theme that is appearing with increasing frequency in the books and publications concerned with the challenges of managing organisations in the twenty-first century. The rise of interest in complexity is a reflection of the modern world, where the advances in information technology and shifts in economic geography have increased the number of pressure points to which managers and leaders need to respond. To quote Peter Senge (2006, page 69), 'perhaps for the first time in history, humankind has the capacity to create far more information than anyone can absorb, to foster far greater interdependency anyone can manage, and to accelerate change far faster than anyone's ability to keep pace'. Coping with complexity requires a different kind of thinking.

To understand why this is important it is first necessary to distinguish a complex project from one that is merely complicated. Let us start with the *simple* project. It involves completing a sequence of tasks with which we are familiar, where both the outcome we expect and the methodology used to get there are entirely predictable. As a project grows in size and duration, it starts to become more complicated. *Complicated* projects will typically have a much higher technical specification and will require input from more people. They have more interacting components but they operate to a *discernible pattern*. We know what should happen because we have seen the pattern before, either on this project or on previous similar projects.

Complex projects are distinguished by the increased number of variables that impact on each stage of the decision-making process. Gokce Sargut and Rita McGrath (2009) identify three features of complexity:

1. Multiplicity – A high level of interacting elements.

2. Interdependence – Individuals relying on the work of others to complete their own tasks.

3. Diversity – project completion requires a diverse range of professional and technical backgrounds.

The greater the degree that each of these elements exists within a project, the more complex it becomes. It is not that the linear sequence of tasks that need to be completed no longer applies, but that the precise inputs that are required from the different experts can no longer be easily predicted. There is no longer a pattern that we can use to predict the outcome. There comes a point when there is too much information for the human brain to manage. Sargut and McGrath make the important observation that we typically overestimate our capacity to take in and make sense of the data each of us as individuals can absorb. Gratton and Erickson (2007) offer a more broadly defined approach to recognising complexity. In their study of collaborative teams, they identified eight possible conditions that are likely to create uncertainty within a group:

1. The task is unlikely to be accomplished successfully using only the skills within an existing team.

2. The task must be addressed by a new group formed specifically for this purpose.

3. The task requires collective input from highly specialised individuals.

4. The task requires collective input and agreement from more than 20 people.

5. The members of the team working on the task are in more than two locations.

6. The success of the task is highly dependent on understanding preferences or needs of individuals outside the group.

7. The outcome of the task will be influenced by events that are highly uncertain and difficult to predict.

8. The task must be completed under extreme time pressure.

Their conclusion is that if *more than two* of these statements are true, the task requires the adoption of collaborative techniques to manage the complexity of the interfaces.

The challenge is to recognise the point that the project moves from *complicated* to *complex*. The pace of change in the modern world creates situations where the features identified above are becoming increasingly present in projects of all sizes. As complexity increases, the team need to see the project less as a series of sequential tasks and more as a 'system', in which each of the project participants undertakes their work according to a set of behavioural norms.

There is an important commercial driver to make this distinction around pricing. External delivery contractors often claim that their real skill is less around the service they provide, and more about their ability to price risk. This makes sense on *complicated* contracts because an experienced contractor will be able to recognise the patterns and price accordingly. One of the primary features of *complex* projects, however, is that the patterns do not exist or are difficult to observe early in the project. It is therefore much more difficult to price with any degree of accuracy. The story tends to play out in one of two ways. Either the sponsor incurs a financial penalty, paying for variations and changes on a time and materials basis, or the contractor makes a loss, because the commitments made were foolhardy. Either way, both sponsor and contractor walk away from the project with a strong sense of dissatisfaction. They are unlikely to work together again.

Traditional project management systems rely on sequential planning tools, which may work well for complicated projects but are less well suited to handling complexity. Managing complex projects requires a further dimension to the project management toolkit – the ability to understand and manage relationships. Complex projects require the core team to become adept at constantly reviewing progress to date and adjusting their plans as new information becomes available. Getting a group of individuals to work in this way requires a different type of project leadership.

Sometimes it may only be part of the project that is complex, for example when there are multiple stakeholders with competing interests. Once a mechanism has been found to accommodate the various interest groups, the delivery of the project itself may be quite straightforward. My point remains however that to manage complexity, even of a small component of a project, still requires a different approach.

Human Ingenuity

On complex projects, problems frequently arise that have not been dealt with before. There is no textbook to turn to or specialist to consult. The team has no option but to try and access the most potentially powerful, yet often neglected, resource that is known as human ingenuity. Ingenuity is defined as the quality of *being clever, original and inventive*. It is the attribute that has allowed the human species to evolve and adapt to be able to survive in every part of our planet.

In the context of a major project, ingenuity is less about innovation and more about enabling progression. It is the ideas and actions that enable the team to find shortcuts and workarounds to challenges that were not anticipated at the start of the project. It could be seen as a free resource, in that it is not a quality that you can specifically buy or hire. It sits within each of us, and therefore potentially within every team.

Thomas Homer-Dixon (2000) coined the phrase 'the ingenuity gap' to describe the space between a challenge and its solution. He explains that the challenge with complex problems is that they are not linear. The traditional 'salami sausage' technique of breaking down a problem into its smaller components is less likely to be successful, in that fixing one part of the problem will often create a new one elsewhere in the system.

Ideas in themselves are not enough to make a difference. It is how those ideas are turned into tangible actions that are the real manifestation of creativity. The power of teams is in the facility to tap into a mix of the skills and attributes of different team members. Creative minds are needed to conceptualise the possibilities but technical minds are also needed to explore the alternative mechanisms for turning potential into reality. It is the mix of the *dreamer* and the *engineer* that actually creates something new.

The challenge is that ingenuity does not necessarily reveal itself unless the conditions are right. Studies confirm that innovation or creativity rarely occur when we are stressed. We know that human beings manage personal risk by reverting to fight or flight mode so the key to unlocking this creative resource is to create the right team *climate.* The implication for the project leader is that you must create an atmosphere where people feel safe to articulate and explore thoughts and ideas in the knowledge that they will be received without ridicule or dismissal.

Transactional versus Coaching Leadership Styles

All projects need leaders. A team will require at least one member to take responsibility for creating a sense of order to the group's activities. How the team performs will be a direct result of the style that the leader choses to adopt. Some individuals are very comfortable in a leadership role, whilst others will actively shy away from such responsibility. There are many possible definitions but, in the context of this discussion, leadership can be thought of as 'the complex interaction between leaders and followers, focusing on relationships, interactions and subjective perception' (Yukl, 2001). As the scope for complexity and ambiguity increases, the need for leadership becomes essential to project success.

Leadership is a good example of a systemic continuum. At one end we have a transactional leadership style which is task-oriented and based on the completion of rational processes. At the other end of the scale is a collaborative style which Bernard Bass (1990) termed 'transformational' leadership, where the leader is able to bring about positive changes in their followers attitudes, perceptions and expectations. Anna Tyssen, Andreas Wald and Patrick Speith (2013) provide a comprehensive review of the research into leadership of temporary organisations and set out the case to be made for adopting a shift from a transactional approach to a transformational style of leadership. Their study considers the output of a wide range of commentators on the subject of leadership and makes a number of observations which are summarised in Table 1.1.

Table 1.1 A comparison of transactional and transformational styles of leadership

Transactional styles are most effective where:	Transformational/collaborative styles are most effective where:
There is strong clarity of the route to goal.	There is uncertainty as to how to achieve the goal.
Short project durations.	Long project durations.
Clear hierarchical structures of authority.	Missing or ambiguous hierarchies.
High degree of familiarity.	High degree of novelty.
Commitment to task completion is sufficient.	There is a strong need for commitment to project performance.
There is a lower perception of uncertainty in the project environment.	There is a higher perception of environmental uncertainty.

The message should be clear. As project complexity increases, leaders need to adopt a transformational approach to leading the team. The problem with such academic papers is that whilst they make a persuasive argument for taking a people-centric approach to project management, they offer little explanation as to how to go about it. For example, just what is a transformational style of leadership? The academics use criteria such as 'charismatic', 'inspirational' and 'visionary'. My problem with such descriptions is that they are personal attributes, rather than choices of behaviour. I have collected many stories of successful projects led by men and women to whom I would ascribe these attributes, but I doubt that any of them would have described themselves as charismatic, visionary or inspirational. On the basis that there are few, if any, legitimate courses in developing one's charisma, I would suggest that the advanced PM should use the term 'people-oriented', and focus on the development of a skill set which helps recognise emotions, personal motivations and intrinsic drivers. These are the key components that underpin the philosophy of team coaching.

Driving or Leading

Does the team leader drive performance or lead it? The word *drive* has a variety of potential meanings. It could mean *steer*, but a more common interpretation is to *urge or force to move in a particular direction*. There is a strong prevalence for inexperienced PMs to see their role as *the force that pushes*. The inference is that other team members lack the will and motivation to do their jobs properly. This reflects a *theory* X view of people.

Douglas McGregor (1960) articulated a cultural difference of approach in organisations. Theory X firms set up their businesses with the underlying belief that the people employed need to be coerced to do their work, that they avoid responsibility and actually preferred to be directed. Theory Y firms in contrast have an underlying belief that given the right environment most people are self-motivated, will use a high degree of creativity and ingenuity, and will actively seek responsibility. One can see that there will be a fundamental difference in values and culture. The choice of values will be driven from the senior management. How these values manifest themselves will differ from business to business, but the impact of either belief system will heavily influence the future work style of young professionals in their twenties as they learn about relationships.

On complex projects I believe that the role of the PM is likely to be more effective if your purpose is to guide and assist rather than goad and intimidate. The problem with the 'rottweiler' approach to project management is that it is based on an assumption that fear is sufficient motivation to move people to take action. As discussed in Chapter 3, humans are not particularly creative when they feel unsafe, as the brain is too absorbed in looking for the sources of danger. Coercive behaviours that intimidate people may produce a short-term burst of activity, but will nearly always result in a collapse of interpersonal trust. Fear has limited use as a tactic if you need to build a collaborative, creative and energetic team.

Peter's Story

I remember one particularly bruising job. The project was a complex refurbishment of a large office building for a major property developer. The client's PM was an ambitious 35-year-old who was rumoured to be next in line for promotion to development director. He seemed to have a very strange idea of how to get people to perform. At every meeting he would publicly and methodically criticise every aspect of each team member's work, often using language that was personally insulting.

The experience was not great. Everybody dreaded coming to the meetings because we just did not know what we were going to be criticised for this time. No one wanted to work on the job and we couldn't wait for it to finish. From memory, the final outcome probably wasn't too bad for the client, although the programme overran by five months, and costs obviously increased. His style clearly didn't go down too well at the development company, and we were quite pleased to hear that he didn't get the promotion.

I think the main thing I learned from the project was never to work with that kind of PM again, and I've always been careful to look for the early warning signs of bullying behaviour since then.

A Coaching Mindset

The second part of this book sets out a number of coaching processes that, when properly implemented, have been shown to establish the optimum framework for collaborative team behaviours. It is important to emphasise the difference between being a team coach and having a coaching mindset. The role of team coach can be seen to be a distinct set of activities that align with, but could be separate from, the team leadership role. On some types of project it might even be worth bringing in an external coach to take on these tasks.

My purpose in writing this book however is to encourage those PMs who sense there is an alternative approach, and to adopt a coaching mindset. This may require the 'unlearning' of many transactional beliefs acquired during your training, as you approach the role as leader from a completely new angle. To illustrate my point, think of the difference between a top-down hierarchical model of management where the leadership role to predict, control and direct.

An alternative is to see the leadership sitting at the base of the hierarchal triangle providing the support the team needs to do their work. My point is that the mindset looking down from the top of the triangle is very different from the perspective to be gained by looking up.

This change in mindset requires a paradigm shift. Paradigm shifts can sometimes occur in a 'light bulb' moment, when you suddenly see things in a different way. At other times the shift occurs slowly as new information is gathered and you start to recognise that your old information is now redundant. Either way, the outcome is a step change in your thinking. This is the essence of new learning.

Summary

In this chapter I have tried to articulate the case for change. My research and my experience reinforce a sense that the continuously changing political, economic and systemic environments in which we live will create ever more complex projects. From which ever angle one looks at the challenge, it is difficult to see how transactional methodologies can be successful. Mindset, however, can be stubborn and slow to adjust to new ways of thinking. It is hard work to change your mind, particularly if your training and your culture encourage you to stay within the perceived safety of transactional thinking. I hope that this chapter has put forward a case for pushing yourself out of your comfort zone and that you are at least open to consider the benefits of adopting a coaching mindset.

Chapter 2

An Introduction to Project Team Coaching

Having made the case for adopting a coaching mindset to managing complex projects, this chapter introduces the concept of team coaching and how, as a PM, you could adjust to an alternative style of working. So what is team coaching? The role of the team coach is relatively new in the context of business but is well established in the field of sport. We are familiar with the idea of an experienced coach who works with a sports team, both as individuals and as a collective entity, to achieve their ultimate objective. The team coach in a work setting can be seen to have a number of similarities, as well as some critical differences.

Within a project team, most members are assumed to be competent in their particular technical discipline. Project team coaching is therefore less concerned about the development of professional skills in the same way that it might be for a footballer or netball player. The emphasis is on filling those gaps in the team process that the team cannot see for themselves. If this explanation is a bit too generic, Table 2.1 summarises how a number of other commentators have defined team coaching.

Table 2.1 Published definitions of team coaching

Author	Vision of team coaching
Perry Zeus and Suzanne Skiffington (2000)	Presents the team coach as a facilitator, helping solve problems, monitoring team performance, and improving communication between the team and their sponsors.
Christine Thornton (2010, page 122)	Describes the exercise as 'coaching a team to achieve a common goal, paying attention to both individual performance and to group collaboration and performance'.
David Clutterbuck (2007)	Regards team coaching as a *learning intervention* designed to increase collective capability and performance of a group or team, through application of the coaching principles of assisted reflection, analysis and motivation for change.

Table 2.1 *continued*

Author	Vision of team coaching
Sir John Whitmore (2003, page 147)	Emphasises the point that 'the basis of coaching to improve team performance is not imposing, but increasing individual and collective awareness and responsibility'.
Peter Hawkins (2011)	Sees team coaching as a *process* by which a team coach works with a whole team, both when they are together and when they are apart, in order to help them improve their collective performance and how they work together.

The value in these definitions is that they illustrate the range of different roles and values that team coaching can provide. Each of the above commentators is regarded as an expert in the field of team coaching. The context of their work is however, primarily focused on the activities of *internal* or *standing teams* rather than projects. The definitions also imply that the role of team coach is separate from team leadership. For the purposes of this book, it is worth adding a distinct definition for *project team coaching* which I would describe is as follows:

> *Project team coaching is the application of a series of interventions that enable a project team to develop and implement the collaborative behaviours required to deliver the desired outcomes of the stakeholders, to the performance standards that the team expect of themselves.*

The salient points in this definition are:

1. The coaching role is enabling rather than directing.
2. The key to *real* teamwork is collaboration.
3. The coach's role is focused on the desired project outcomes, not on the team as individuals.
4. The team decide what their performance standards should be.
5. The role can be part of, or distinct from, the role of project leadership.

In the context of coaching, an *intervention* is an action designed to encourage an individual, or a group, to pause and consider their approach to a problem and assess the alternatives. In most cases, coaching interventions are in the form of questions. The implications of the above definition are covered in more detail in the next few chapters but, as an illustration, some examples of team coaching process include:

- Clarity of objective – Why does this particular team exist?
- Stakeholder relations – What do they expect of us?
- Articulation of the challenge – How will this project stretch us?
- The ground rules – How should we behave when we meet?
- Communications – How will the team members connect with each other and project stakeholders?
- Resolution – How will conflict be managed?
- Reflection – How do we recognise what we are learning from this project experience?

The purpose of definitions is to help distinguish one role or set of activities from another. Project team coaching is not therefore simply about facilitation, team building or process consulting. As discussed later, each of these activities may be a component part of the team coaching role, but in isolation they fail the critical test in that they only address part of the challenge. Project team coaching is primarily concerned with achieving the final goal or outcome, rather than the application of process irrespective of the ultimate results.

Before we consider some of the coaching skills that will be useful, it is worth clarifying just what I mean when I use the term 'team'.

Real Teams and Work Groups

In the course of my research, I was quite surprised by the low level of ambition that so many participants have of a project team. The majority of major projects are set up with the assumption that the people involved will behave as an efficient working group. The client or sponsor assembles a group based on a perception of their experience and capability. In terms of team interaction, the primary expectation is often limited to the sharing of information so that each can provide their component of the pre-designed solution. The prevalent thinking in many industries could be summarised by the simplistic view that 'if everybody turns up and does what they say they will do, the project will run according to plan'. Experience tells us that the reality is more complicated.

The distinction between a *real team* and a *work group* is well established in the literature on team performance. If you are unfamiliar with the concept, then I would recommend that you read Katzenbach and Smith (1993). I have nevertheless included a simple description of the different potential phases of the team's existence in Table 2.2.

Table 2.2 Potential team phases

Project team phase	Progression	Description
Real team	Forwards	A group totally committed to delivering the project where their actions make it clear to the other members that personal success is mutually interdependent. If one members fails, everyone fails.
Potential team	Forwards	A group that starts to recognise the mutual benefit of achieving the goal of project completion and are comfortable sharing information and ideas. Social connections amongst the members are strong and they provide each other with a degree of mutual support. There is however no sense of joint accountability, as each member views their own contribution as being independent.
Work group	Neutral	A group of specialists assembled to work on a project where each individual member is acting as a representative for their home organisation. Whilst there may be a common goal to see the project reach completion, there is no sense of accountability outside of their specialist input.
Transactional team	Backwards	The group members start off as a *work group* that quickly starts to lose efficiency, usually as a result of systemic forces having a negative effect upon interpersonal behaviours.
Dysfunctional team	Backwards	A group whose members are struggling with low levels of interpersonal trust, where communication has become formalised and whose members have disengaged from the project.

Every team starts as a *work group*. It is important to recognise that formation is not a stable state. As illustrated in Figure 2.1, it is possible to imagine that the team comes together for its first meeting on the side of a hill. The gradient of the hill will be a reflection of the external environment and the extent to which the project is subjected to either transactional or collaborative influences.

As the team begin to get to know each other, the group will either start the uphill progression towards becoming a *real team* or they will revert to transactional behaviours and start to slip downwards. Moving in an upwards direction requires effort. Energy needs to be expended at the very start to give the team the initial momentum to build good working relationships and to learn to trust each other.

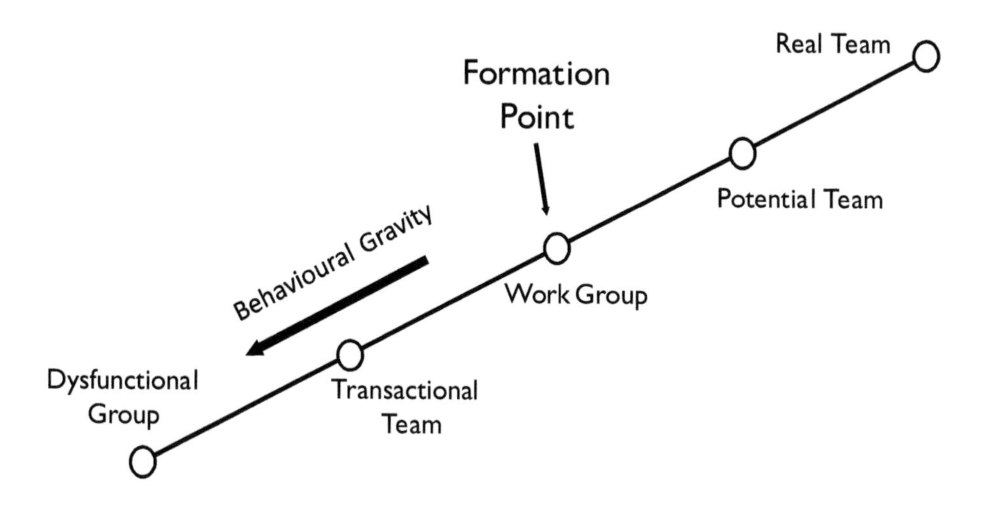

Figure 2.1 Illustration of behavioural gravity on teams

Creating a *real team* therefore requires an investment in time and energy, and often also in hard cash. Sometimes *real teams* emerge quickly from the *work group* phase as the individuals naturally gel and settle into a team dynamic in which they are all comfortable. For complex projects however, this is not something that can be left to chance. If the outcome is important enough, then the investment in setting up the team to adopt the right behaviours is worth making.

When I have discussed the concept of team coaching with a number of PMs, we have found a lot of common agreement on the need to invest in the project set-up process. They will, however, quite often then reflect that it is very difficult to get the project sponsor to pay for this investment. This brings us back to the muddle caused by transactional thinking. Major projects consume a huge amount of resource, so why take the risk of waste and delay, simply because there is a mistaken assumption that everything will be fine. The challenge for an enlightened PM is to influence the project sponsors early on in their engagement to recognise the high value of developing a *real team*. The theme of project set-up and the need for early client engagement is covered in more detail in Chapter 4.

Signs of Dysfunction

Whether or not you or your sponsors believe that the effort expended on project set-up is worthwhile will depend on whether you have experienced trying to work in a team where communication has collapsed. Stories about working on teams that have gone bad tend to feature the following:

- Meetings are tense and few controversial issues are discussed in open forum.
- There is a tendency to revert to contractual obligation.
- Outside of the meeting, communication is by email, and the content is usually focused on avoiding blame or passing it to others in the team.
- Problems are passed up and down the hierarchy as team members avoid ownership.
- Team members become disengaged from the project and put in the minimal effort required to complete their part of the project.

The outcome is virtually always a failure in performance. The project costs escalate and the programme completion is delayed. As for customer satisfaction, you can work that out for yourself.

Process Loss and Process Gain

So what do you expect from your team? Is hard work and a commitment to the cause enough, or do you also want good communication and creative problem solving? The extent to which these behaviours are adopted by your team will depend partly on whether you have the right people in the mix, but more importantly upon the strategies and tactics that you choose to implement from the start of the project. We have established in the previous chapter that complex projects are not well suited to the learned behaviours associated with transactional thinking. For projects that must deal with complexity, we need teams to be more than the sum of their parts. We need two plus two to equal five. Researchers into team dynamics call this *process gain*.

Process gain is a phenomenon that occurs when the output from the group working as a team is greater than could be achieved by individuals working alone. An alternative word is 'synergy'. The problem with *synergy* is that it is an ethereal concept. What specifically are we seeking? Is it about quicker task completion, better problem solving and decision making, or simply the motivation of others in the team to produce their best work? The answer could be all of these and more. The reality is that a team will only be able to recognise that they have achieved synergy in hindsight. They are unlikely to be aware of it at the time, as everyone is too absorbed in the delivery of the project.

There is an opposite to process gain which is more easily recognisable. *Process loss* occurs where the dynamics of a team are disruptive and actually hinder progress. The output of the team is therefore lower when the group is working together than could be achieved by individuals who are working alone. The evidence from many team studies is not encouraging, and the odds are stacked in favour of a suboptimal result. Many reasons have been identified to explain why process loss occurs:

- mismatch of personalities;
- lack of attention to team structure and procedure;
- lack of leadership;
- mismatch of aspirations;
- low levels of interpersonal trust;
- fear of humiliation;
- lack of commitment.

This is not simply a matter of team members failing to collaborate because they do not like each other. Process loss often occurs because the system in which the team is operating creates unnecessary pressures, which reduce trust and increase tension. On transactional contracts, process loss is the normal state in which the team members work. When transactional projects fail, as they frequently do, the cause is usually attributed to an individual rather than the system itself.

J. Richard Hackman and Ruth Wageman (2005) established a concept of team coaching which recognises that, whilst interpersonal problems are often a feature of under performing teams, it is a lack of focus on the core components of team performance that will often cause interpersonal issues to come to the surface. They identify three core performance processes where a coach can have an impact on team effectiveness:

1. motivate the team to increase the level of effort expended;
2. advise the team on their performance strategies;
3. help the team extend their knowledge and skills.

They set out the useful concept that team coaching is specifically focused on those interventions that 'inhibit process losses and foster process gains for each of the three performance processes'. An important point that emerges from their work is that the role of the coach is to identify and contain bad team behaviours as much as it is to encourage good behaviour. These performance processes will vary according to the needs of the project. This is a judgement call that improves with experience.

Dual Role of Team Leader and Team Coach

Is it possible to be both the team leader and the team coach? The answer depends upon your perspective or mindset. If you see the role of the PM sitting distinctly within the activities that are prescribed in the standard PM methodologies, then it may be difficult to take the next step up. If, on the other hand, you recognise that complex projects require an alternative management strategy, then adding coaching methodologies to your repertoire will make sense.

When I looked at my notes from the stories collected as part of my research, it was interesting to see how frequently my interviewees were able to identify a project where the leader had used an approach that involved some or all of the coaching techniques described later in this book. They did not think of themselves as having two different roles. It was simply the most logical way of managing a difficult project.

Nick's Story

I remember that the project came together rapidly. This was not a large project, only about £3 million, but it was a complicated refurbishment that needed to be done to an accelerated programme. In the past I have worked on lots of projects where I would walk into the room and know lots of people on the team as I would have worked with them before. In this particular case I had not met any of the people before. I remember that we felt at ease with each other very quickly. I was the cost consultant on the project at the time and I remember thinking that the PM was quite enigmatic. He had a lot of flair but also seemed to be an easy-going person. He was not a 'bang the table' PM at all. He had a very collaborative style. His introduction was simply 'we need to do this project quickly guys, so let's all pull together and make it work'.

I can see now that the PM was also the team coach. He was the one who understood the client's dilemma, and was charged with getting them out of the problem. But he was the also the one who had to explain the brief and set out just what we had to achieve. He managed to pull everyone along with him and made us work as a team.

Team Coaching as a Philosophy

My proposition is that any PM working with complexity will benefit from learning a number of the basic skill sets used by a team coach. For some PMs these skills may be 'bolt-ons' to your existing methodology, to be used as and when they might be appropriate. For others, they represent a paradigm shift where the project management process becomes inverted and their modus operandi changes from the sequential, task completion model to a more holistic version where people, task and process orientations are all intertwined. Over time this paradigm shift starts to become embedded in your own personal working philosophy.

A philosophy can be thought of as a set of values and principles that set your criteria for day-to-day decision making. There are five elements that I believe form the basis of good project team coaching philosophy:

1. slow down to speed up;
2. think systemically;
3. use influence over persuasion;
4. ask questions and then listen;
5. look below the surface.

1. SLOW DOWN TO SPEED UP

One of the consistent components of the coaching role is to encourage the team to collectively take the time to pause to work through alternative options and then decide on the optimum solution. John McQuire and Vance Tang (2011) observe that urgency, uncertainty and complexity create situations in which managers feel that they have lost control. In their desire to gain clarity, managers try to move faster only to find that they have created more uncertainty. McQuire and Tang put forward the idea that complex problems require 90 per cent enquiry and 10 per cent decision making. The point is that not only do you need to collect the necessary data surrounding the problem but you also need the time to think through what the data is really telling you.

Slow thinking is hard work. Daniel Kahneman (2011) writes about the tendency of human beings to rely on instinctive (thinking fast) judgement over rational analysis (thinking slow). His explanation is that thinking actually requires a lot of energy and so, when we are tired or under pressure, we revert to the easier cognitive mechanisms. Relying on our intuition may help us make decisions quickly but it does not mean that we then produce the optimum result. Kahneman makes the case that what we might think of as intuition is not some mystic force but is instead the ability to tap into the unconscious memories of events that we have previously experienced or have learned from others. Errors in judgement occur when we try to apply our intuition to situations that are outside of our experience, as will typically occur when problems move from complicated to complex.

Slow thinking requires checking our biases and assumptions, and acknowledging that there may be additional information that needs to be considered. In the project arena, slow thinking has the greatest impact at the start, when plans are being worked up. Slow thinking is also valuable as the team goes about the process of project delivery, reinforcing good behaviours and building resilience for those times when the project is struggling with change and a lack of resources. When you are under pressure to hit deadlines or even to just be seen to be active, it can be counterintuitive to slow down. The coaching role is to provide the voice that says 'let's just take some time out to think about this one'.

2. THINK SYSTEMICALLY

The next philosophical element is recognition of the need to look beyond the immediately obvious and consider the factors that sit behind the situation or issue. The concept is often called systemic thinking or systems thinking and is based on the idea that everything is somehow connected to everything else. The starting point is to recognise that we rarely operate in isolation but instead work as part of a system (or variety of systems). A system comprises a set of interconnected activities that are created and are then continuously adapted by human beings. Our behaviour will be strongly influenced by the systems in which we operate. Pete Senge (2006) describes systemic thinking as a way of seeing the structures that underlie complex situations. An event may appear to have been caused by a particular sequence of actions but, in reality, the cause extends beyond the evidence that we observe at first glance. Systems theory prompts the investigator to look at all of the other influential factors that exist in the system in which the event occurred.

Systemic thinking helps recognise why some organisations seem to manage to satisfy customers, staff and shareholders effortlessly whilst similar firms consistently struggle to get it right. It is a matter of looking past the organisation's processes and procedures, and seeking to understand how behaviours are shaped by a collective set of vision and values. My partners, Will Karlsen and Adrian Wheeler (2014) at the Fairlight Project have come up with a visual graphic that helps illustrate the concept of what they have termed the 'Spheres of Influence' (see Figure 2.2). Each sphere represents a different aspect of a person's interaction with their organisation either at a personal, interpersonal or team level. The organisation also sits within a wider sphere in which it must react and interact with its stakeholders. In trying to understand why an individual or even a team is behaving irrationally, the systemic approach allows one to consider the influence that all five spheres maybe having on the situation.

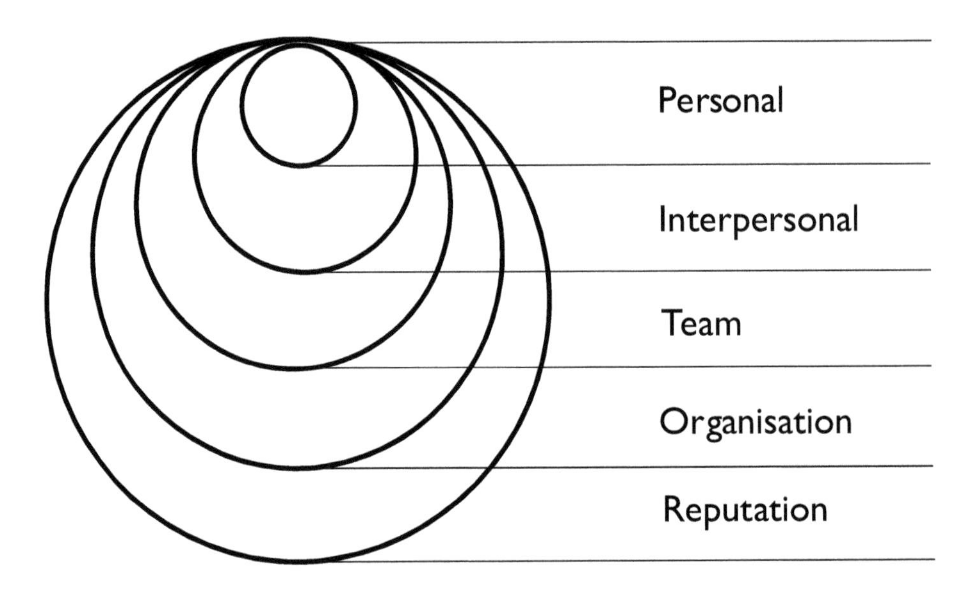

Figure 2.2 The Spheres of Influence
Source: With permission from Karlsen and Wheeler.

The model provides a useful way of looking for other perspectives that may be relevant or influential on the specific issue or problem. It is a mechanism to prompt the secondary questions that may help reveal deeper issues. Take, for example, a communication problem between the team and an individual representing the project sponsor. Walking away from an angry exchange, you might be tempted to dismiss the other person as being inadequate for their role. A systemic approach, however, would also consider the following questions:

- Are there other issues that may be affecting their attitude that are not connected with the project?
- Is this a personal clash or misunderstanding between the two of us?
- Are we as a team failing to explain our challenges in a way that our sponsoring body can understand?
- Are there changes going on in the dynamics of the wider organisation that we are not yet aware of?
- Are there pressures coming from outside of the organisation that are creating pressures on the team?

Your answers to these questions will usually create a requirement to seek further information and should help you see other aspects of the interrelationships between the team and also with the project sponsor.

3. USE INFLUENCE OVER PERSUASION

Persuasion is a process of applying coercive forces that create pressure for another party to change their position, sometimes physically but more often in what they *think*. These forces can be subtle or aggressive. In most cases, our purpose is to try and get another person, or group of people, to see a situation from our perspective. It is usually done with benign intent. Persuasive people often use their passion and energy to try and enforce the belief that their view of the world is the correct one. In the face of an irresistible force the recipient will often accede and appear to have shifted their thinking. The problem with persuasion is that it relies on the maintenance of pressure. Once the pressure is removed, our thoughts and behaviours are likely to revert to their original position. To achieve a paradigm shift you have to allow your counterpart to make his or her own mental journey to reach that perspective.

Influence, therefore, is the process of helping people arrive at a similar view to our own, but by allowing them to reach the conclusion through their own mental filters. Developing your influencing skills requires one significant conceptual leap, which is to start every crucial conversation with the assumption that you do not have all the information needed to help someone else understand your perspective. You therefore need to work through an activity which Stephen R. Covey (1992) describes as 'seek first to understand, then be understood'.

The essence of team coaching is to first understand each member of your team so that you can connect and communicate with them in such a way that they understand you. This is a simple concept and, as such, it is easy to pay limited attention to what this really means. Once you get this concept embedded in the way that you work, it can be a powerful way of influencing your colleagues. Do not, however, underestimate how difficult it is to break the conditioning of your project management training. The instinct of many PMs is to *tell* others what needs to be done and then *ignore* most of the potential information that comes back in response.

4. ASK QUESTIONS AND THEN LISTEN

Questions form the basis of human communication. They are your primary mechanism for building relationships with your team. The extent to which each individual is prepared to trust you to lead them will be influenced by the questions that you use to build rapport with them at the start of the project. We think of questions as a technique for exchanging information but they are just as often used as a way of attempting to control a conversation. Leading questions that have an obvious answer can draw your listener down a particular line of thought. Rhetorical questions are often used as a mechanism for the reinforcement of a singular point of view. Both are used in the tactics of persuasion and are of little use if your intention is to try and understand the other person. Questions can often be confrontational or accusatory, or can be interpreted as such if you use a particular tone of voice or inflection.

To influence, you first need to comprehend how someone is thinking. What are the 'lenses' that they are using to make sense of their world and how do they differ from yours? It is useful to check the assumptions you are making about the situation and what new information there might be that can help you get a clearer understanding of the issue as they see it.

This may be a challenging proposition. As Ed Schein (2013) points out, we live in a culture of 'Do and Tell', where task accomplishment is valued more than relationship building. It can be seen as a response to the perceived wisdom that success is attached to speed of action, whilst trying to maintain a degree of control. It is another symptom of a transactional mindset. Schein advocates the use of 'humble enquiry' which he defines as, 'The fine art of drawing someone out, and asking questions to which you do not already know the answer, of building a relationship based on curiosity and interest in the other person.' He chooses the word *humble* to emphasise the need to break out of the hierarchical mindset and expose oneself to the other party as needing help. His observation is that such exposure is often the first step in building interpersonal trust.

'Really' listening

The flip side of asking questions is then to listen to the response. For many people, listening is simply a pause for breath whilst they think about what they are going to say next. You may therefore require a reset in the normal way that you practice listening. Absorbing the available information requires taking in *all* of the signals, which will include the words that are said, how they are phrased, the tone of voice used and the body language of the speaker. This is considerably more data than you are likely to consciously take in when you are in 'directing' mode. You therefore need to recognise your own tendency not to really listen and instead concentrate on the different sources of data being presented to you. This process is sometimes called 'active' listening and there are a range of techniques that could come under this heading. I believe that the four most useful components are:

1. Pay attention
   Focus on what the person is saying, not on your own thoughts and possible solutions or responses. Try not to allow your mind to wander off onto other matters. If you become distracted, you will miss several parts of messages that are being communicated. Worse than that, the speaker will instinctively recognise that you're no longer listening and will lose concentration herself.

2. Listen with your eyes
   The eyes are the basic indicator that you are paying attention. When trying to solve a problem many people will look away, to the side or to the ceiling. This is a sign that they are thinking, not that they had lost interest in the conversation. As the listener, however, you should keep your eyes focused on the face of the speaker. Not only will this help you pick out signals around body posture, and the pitch and pace of their voice, but it will tell the speaker that you are totally concentrating on what they have to say. Research shows that by maintaining contact on the face of the speaker you will significantly enhance their capacity to think through an issue.

3. Don't interrupt
   If you reflect on your own experience, when you're trying to explain your thinking, how useful is it when the other person interrupts before you are ready? Most people need to say things out loud before they fully make sense to themselves. Just when they are about to make a critical connection that joins up all of the disconnected thoughts around a problem, you jump in with ideas and thoughts of your own. The other person may now be silent and you think that they are listening to you. It is more likely that they are desperately trying to find a connection that has now disappeared and will not remember the point that you're now making. So allow the speaker the time to work through their thoughts. This may even require allowing for a short period of silence. If you get the listening right you will often create a situation where the speaker is really

thinking more clearly than they could have done by themselves. It is therefore important to remember that just because they had stopped talking does not mean that they have completed the full cognitive process. You should be able to tell whether they are ready to continue the conversation by the expression on their face and whether their eyes are in focus. So allow for some quiet space and do not be tempted to jump in and 'fill the silence'.

4. Be sparing with your advice
   It is particularly difficult for an experienced PM not to give advice on what they believe the correct answer should be. Remember that the underlying theory of influence is that most people will put more effort, energy and creativity into implementing an idea that they feel they have found on their own, rather than an idea that has been imposed upon them. Of the disciplines that make up the practice of really listening, holding back your advice is probably the hardest one to learn. If you have some information that may be useful to the speaker, save it until the end of the conversation.

Don't fall into the common practice of listening to reply. To understand, you need to try and work out what the speaker is trying to communicate and what their motivations are. Remember that we cannot read other peoples' minds, and so you should not assume that because you have come across a similar situation before, you understand their thoughts feelings and motivations.

5. LOOK BELOW THE SURFACE

'So what is going on here?' is a question that you should learn to habitually ask yourself. It is an internal enquiry that prompts you to look below the surface. You are looking for the clues that may reveal the underlying psychological factors that help explain the team's actions and behaviours. I am not advocating that you try to become an amateur psychologist, but an understanding of the basic factors that influence human behaviour are going to be very helpful in recognising the forces that will help to explain why some teams work and others do not. This is the subject of the next chapter.

Summary

In the second part of this book, I set out a broad range of activities that could be applied by an individual working as a consultant coach to the team. As an independent party they could undertake the series of tasks that would improve the ability of the team and its stakeholders to work effectively together. My belief, however, is that with the right attitude or mindset there is no reason why a PM cannot implement most of the tasks that might otherwise be left to an external specialist.

The point that I have tried to emphasise in this chapter is that by taking the time to slow down and look at the team from a systemic and a behavioural point of view, you can find a new set of solutions to problems that you may have previously tried to ignore. My observation is that the more that you see these tasks as part of the philosophy of the way that you work, the more effective you are likely to be in your role. This will take time and practise, and there will be times when the transactional forces are simply too strong to try and experiment with a new approach. The need to manage complexity, however, is more likely to grow as we move further into the twenty-first century. Time invested in developing your coaching capabilities is unlikely to be wasted.

Before we move into the detail and explore a model project team coaching, there is another step in this learning journey. To coach a team you need to recognise what is going on beneath the surface of the team's day-to-day interactions, and the psychological factors that influence both your own behaviour and that of your team. This is the subject of the following chapter.

Chapter 3
An Introduction to the Psychology of Teams

As we have previously discussed, complex projects are defined by the number of potential variables that are difficult to plan or predict. Since human behaviour is one of the most unpredictable of these variables, it is worth trying to assemble whatever information is available that might help us understand the factors that affect patterns of behaviour. This chapter provides a brief introduction to some of the observations, theories and practices from the fields of psychiatry and psychology that have an effect on how people successfully work together in a group.

When we watch a group of people interacting, our observations are often based on superficial information. We tend to focus on the content of what is being said, and ignore most of the other information that is being transmitted and received. To understand what is going on in your team, it helps to recognise the other factors that contribute to a team's dynamics. The word *dynamics* is often used to describe the way that a number of people interact with each other, but what it actually means is the 'forces of change'. Group dynamics are the observable outcome of the exchanges that are going on in a team, the causes of which are not immediately apparent. 'So what is going on here?' is perhaps one of the most important questions that project team coaches should keep asking themselves. The role requires that you see what others may not necessarily be able to see. It is the activity that sits below the surface that begs such questions as:

1. Why does he keep behaving this way?
2. Why does she keep doing that when it clearly doesn't work?
3. Why do some of the team click and others don't?

4. Why is she so defensive?

5. Why did that meeting with the client go really well?

We cannot read other people's minds, although we often make assumptions that we can. A better strategy is to recognise that the signals we receive are little more than clues to the real factors that are generating the behaviours that we observe. A basic understanding of human psychology will help to decipher the code and enable us to have a better idea of what is going on when the team just don't seem to be working well together.

Fight or Flight versus Creativity

A useful starting point in the exploration of human psychology is a recognition that all human beings are wired to respond very quickly to any situation that we perceive to be threatening to ourselves or others that we are close to. A basic survival instinct kicks in as we subconsciously choose between fight, flight or freeze. Whatever behavioural traits you can see in yourself or observe in others, it is important to understand that in a threatening situation 'all bets are off', and we will do whatever we feel we need to do to look after ourselves or our tribe. The likelihood of physical harm is unusual in most project environments. More common is a threat to our sense of identity or self-esteem. This is complicated, largely because it is invisible. We don't really understand other people's sensitivities until we get to know them. We only discover how volatile or resilient others are when the pressure starts to build and team members become less cautious about the ways that they express themselves.

Our understanding of the human mind is changing as new technology allows scientists and psychologists to understand the physiological changes that occur in our brains in response to different stimuli. The rapidly expanding field of neuroscience is generating a great deal of interest, not just in the medical world but also in business. Advances in technology are now providing a scientific explanation for those things that we have observed in ourselves and others but often discount because we do not understand them. We can now track those parts of the brain that are active in different situations and which chemicals have been released in response to different opportunities and threats. Jan Hills (2014) highlights a study by the University of Wisconsin, which identified that whilst fear makes people more alert, it interferes with the ability to use the upper regions of the brain that deal with planning and decision making.

Team meetings that have an underlying tension between individuals will therefore rarely be as productive as sessions where every member feels both physically and psychologically safe.

Peter Robertson (2005) set out a useful summary of two basic human drivers in his exploration of *ethology* or 'comparative behavioural studies'. His work examines the concepts that have been developed around the behaviours that arise from the survival instincts which compel us to first form *attachments* and to then *explore*. Human beings, in common with most mammals, are genetically coded to find safety by attaching themselves to something. For most mammals, our first attachment is to our mother, but studies show that in the absence of a caring parent we can also potentially find this attachment in inanimate objects.

As we grow older, humans continue to have the need for the security that comes from attachment. This can apply to an organisation or quite often to a project. The purpose of adult attachment is to find something that provides us with an element of certainty and control. When this security is in place, humans will then seek to explore. The theory is that exploration is also a hardwired mechanism for survival, in that our ancestors needed to keep extending the boundaries of their known territory to find new resources. Attachment and exploration theory may be an overly simplistic analysis of human complexity but there is sufficient accuracy in the underlying thinking for us to be able to recognise the impact of these two powerful motivators. The obvious learning from this theory is that, as the team leader/coach, if you want to establish a creative and collaborative team, you need to put in place those things that will allow your colleagues to find attachment to the safety of their experiences of the team so that they naturally start to explore.

Human beings are nevertheless highly adaptable and can become used to working in some very difficult environments once they have managed to rationalise any potential threats. Managing complexity becomes much easier once you acquire an ability to become comfortable with ambiguity and uncertainty. It is a mental paradigm or mindset that is able to accept that whilst change is inevitable, you have the skills and support that will be needed to find a way through whatever problems are likely to arise. This mindset is initially difficult to acquire but can be developed over time. It becomes much easier when you have trust in your colleagues.

Building Trust

As discussed in Chapter 2, when a team comes together for the first time they start as a *work group*. They are not a *real team* until they understand how they will go about achieving the team's goals and how they need to interact to succeed. Each member then needs to go through the process of learning to trust the other members. Trust is a fundamental requirement of any relationship that needs to move beyond the transactional mindset. In the context of a project we are silently asking ourselves:

> *'Can you deliver your part of the package?'*
>
> *'Will you turn up when you say you will?'*
>
> *'Do you mean what you say?'*
>
> *'Will you hold it together when things get tough?'*
>
> *'Will you back me up when we have to deliver a difficult message?'*

Trust is a personal decision. It is also a conscious rather than unconscious phenomenon. We can quickly say whether we trust someone or not. It is also a matter of degree, in that we can trust someone to do some things but not necessarily others. You might trust a colleague to be technically capable of undertaking her assignment but not necessarily to go out of her way to support you when you are under pressure.

On the other hand, trust can also be systemic. Some firms place a lot of trust in an individual to take a project and move it forward with minimal supervision. Other organisations institutionalise a distrust of their staff by imposing processes and procedures that are designed to limit the ability of an individual to make decisions. Systemic trust inevitably affects the environment in which the team operates. Transactional environments require low levels of interpersonal trust, and so behaviours often default to a position where people have low expectations of reciprocation. If one individual shows self-focused behaviours, self-preservation will move us to match those behaviours or to seek to disengage from the team. For a collaborative group to form, the participants need to see and hear that transactional behaviours are inappropriate. They need to recognise, very early in the group's formation, that a different approach is required when they interact with others in the team.

Trust within a team develops over time, as we watch and listen to our colleagues to see if their values match our own. We want to see whether they actually do what they say they are going to do. *Work groups* that do not learn to trust each other cannot progress to becoming a team. For a PM in a hurry to get the team established, this can be frustrating. The speed at which we develop trust will vary according to our internal motivation system. As discussed later in this chapter, some people have a strong motivation to build and maintain interpersonal relationships. Others have a low in-built need to work with colleagues, and so may take longer to form the bonds that create trust. We are also more inclined to trust people that we believe understand us and are much more suspicious of individuals who we feel do not understand our point of view.

Stephen M.R. Covey (2006) believes that trust can be accelerated. He identifies a need to firstly take time to assess your own level of credibility, based on your integrity, intent, capability and track record. These are the factors that others will judge you on. He then advocates the consistent application of a series of open behaviours that reveal your own values. He believes that it is also important that you are willing to understand the values and beliefs of others. Examples of open behaviour would include creating transparency, listening first, loyalty, keeping commitments and showing respect.

A lack of trust slows a project down. It is not difficult to see the difference in progress that can be made by a team who are prepared to believe in each other's capabilities and integrity, and those where every action is potentially open to question. On complex projects, trust is the critical factor that distinguishes success from failure. Creating the right environment to accelerate the development of trust is a core component of the team coaching role. The activities that can help establish this environment are set out in the next chapter. First however, it is worth exploring some of the other factors that affect team dynamics.

Forming and Storming

Bruce Tuckman (1965) established the now familiar model of the four stages of team development, these being *forming, storming, norming* and *performing*. The model recognises that people in new groups need to go through a period of testing each other out to establish the 'pecking order'. His proposition is that groups need to understand this relative positioning before they can settle into their collective tasks. As William Schutz (1958) identifies, when a person joins a new group, he or she is open to learning a new set of behaviours according to their particular need for *inclusion, control* and *affection*. Our first instinct is to work out whether we are going to be included in the group. This is a response to a fundamental need to gain security from the recognition and acceptance of others. Once we feel that we are 'inside' rather than 'outside' the group, our concern switches to an assessment of the degree to which we want to control, or are prepared to be controlled by, others in the group. Some people have a strong need to have the dominant position in any relationship and will seek to be influential. Others have a greater need for independence and will resent any attempt to limit how they work.

The *forming* and *storming* stages therefore involve each individual looking for signals from the other members to decide if being a part of the group is going to be a positive or negative experience. It is not always an obvious phenomenon and may not even present itself in some teams. A study by Connie Gersick (1988) found that some teams did not follow Tuckman's four-phase structure, observing that each team established their working methodologies quite quickly and then pressed on with their tasks. There is, however, sufficient evidence in other studies of team dynamics to recognise that many groups need to go through a phase of testing each other before settling into a routine work pattern. Much depends on the project environment. The *storming* phase is more likely to occur in teams formed from *internal* resources, where hierarchies are less obvious than *external* teams where each member joins the team with a specific role.

Where the *storming* phase occurs, it is likely to have an influence on the initial cohesion of the team. Tuckman describes this stage as the period when the team members compete to establish where they sit in relation to each other. Early team business may be ineffective as conclusions to any discussion are slow to form. There may also be several challenges to your leadership, testing to see if you are up to the job. Recognising these dynamics is useful, as you may be in a hurry to work through your agenda, but the group's subconscious attention is elsewhere. To establish some order in the early meetings is important to have a clear goal as to what you wish to achieve so that you can keep the attention on the vision and mission of the project.

The *storming* phase can therefore be quite unsettling for any leader, irrespective of their age or experience, because you don't know exactly what is going to happen. It helps to accept that it is a natural human process, but that it should not be allowed to disrupt the establishment of good team process. As project coach, your role is to manage the early interactions so that a collaborative behavioural model is established. Left to the law of the jungle, it is quite easy for dominant personalities to establish an environment where the less extroverted individuals decide not to engage with the project.

An Introduction to Psychometrics

We tend to look at human behaviour as a random process, where everyone is different. We think of ourselves as being unique. Careful observation, however, reveals that our behaviours are more consistent that you might think. We can easily recognise the different traits that distinguish people working in the creative professions from those working in the more logical and precise roles that are common in areas such as accountancy and engineering. We can look around us and see how people have different perspectives on similar issues. For thousands of years, wise men and women have understood that people tend to share similar tendencies. The ancient Greeks used the four humours – sanguine, phlegmatic, choleric and melancholic to explain perceived differences in personality. In the last 50 years or so psychologists have started to create tests which can be used to predict how different individuals might react to the same external stimulus. We can be categorised or profiled.

One of the major implications of our psychological profile is that two people may have an identical experience, but will interpret the event differently according to the filters through which they see the world. The peculiar thing, however, is that despite the evidence that is presented to us, we still have trouble adjusting to the reality that others do not use the same logical pathway to form an opinion on the same matter. In other words, we still expect everyone to think as we do. Recognising this phenomenon is important if you need to make better connections with other people to achieve your purpose. Numerous experts in human behaviour have developed different mechanisms to test the factors that affect our behaviour, commonly referred to as *psychometric* tests. These tests also illustrate our differences from the other population segments, helping us to understand why 'everyone may not actually think like me'.

The use of psychometrics has grown significantly over the last 20 years, initially as a development tool to improve self-awareness, then as a recruitment accessory. As managers have become more comfortable with the concept they have used them to develop their operational teams. They are now also becoming more commonly used in the development of project teams. There are hundreds of different tests, usually based on an online questionnaire that then generates a report showing the individual's scores and their possible implications.

Most of the tests claim to have a credible theoretical basis, although the barrier to entry in terms of creating your own questionnaire is quite low. If someone is selling their own proprietary test or 'inventory', it is always worth asking them to provide some further detail on the theory that underpins their system.

The following section reviews the three common theoretical structures used in the more established psychometric methodologies that are relevant to team development:

1. personality type
2. personality traits
3. motivational value systems (MVS).

PERSONALITY TYPE

Swiss psychiatrist, Carl Jung, developed a theory of personality *type* in the 1920s. Type theory is based on the concept that people have a natural preference towards specific ways in which they use their perception and judgement. Jung's theory was later developed by Katherine Myers and Isabel Briggs into one of the most commonly used psychometric testing tools know as the Myers Briggs Type Indicator or MBTI (Myers, 1998). This tool looks at four dichotomous distinctions:

1. Extroversion versus Introversion
2. Sensing versus Intuition
3. Thinking versus Feeling
4. Judging versus Perceiving

A short description of these preferences is set out in Table 3.1.

Table 3.1 Descriptions of Myers Briggs Type Indicator (MBTI) preferences

Extraversion (E)	**Introversion (I)**
People with strong E preference tend to get the stimulation from the external environment. They like variety of action and are often sociable. Recognition and approval from others are important, and they can be quite focused on achieving results. This preference can reveal a tendency to be impatient, dislike tedious jobs involving detail. Decision making is often impulsive rather than considered.	A strong I preference indicates a desire for self-sufficiency and the time and space to think things through. They are comfortable with detail and show patience with long projects. The downside can be a tendency for procrastination and a low need for communication with others.
Sensing (S)	**Intuition (N)**
A strong S score indicates someone who prefers to make decisions based on known facts and likes to work through a problem in a logical and methodical manner. They are often impatient when presented with unproven ideas and possibilities, and distrust decisions based on intuition or inspiration.	People with a strong N score tend to focus their thinking on the bigger picture, and are often imaginative and verbally creative. They trust their intuition and move quickly to conclusions.
Thinking (T)	**Feeling (F)**
A T preference indicates someone who likes to analyse and put events into a logical order. They are less concerned with the feelings of others and can be dispassionate in their decision making.	An F preference is illustrated by empathy and values based decision making. They have a need to respond to the feelings and values of others. People with a strong F preference like harmony and will try to avoid conflict where possible.
Judging (J)	**Perceiving (P)**
A high J score indicates a preference for making plans and having a high degree of predictability in their lifestyle. Js often have a low level of flexibility and will resist changing a decision once it is made.	A P score reflects a desire for spontaneity and flexibility. They like to leave decisions open to change, and will react quickly to new information.

MBTI is probably the best known of all of the psychometric tests. It is relatively easy to understand and has been found by many people to be a useful starting point for developing self-awareness. Critics argue that it lacks any clear scientific foundation, but its validation comes from the thousands of sceptical managers who take test and are surprised by the apparent insights that the MBTI report is able to generate. The system is then propagated as they introduce the test to others in their team. It estimated that roughly 2,500,000 people in North America take the MBTI every year, making it the most commonly used of all of the psychometric tools.

MBTI is also open to criticism that it puts people in a category or box, and therefore does not readily allow for variations that arise in different environments. Whilst many MBTI practitioners also claim that it is a great team development tool, it can sometimes be overcomplicated if you only have a short amount of time to introduce the test and its results to the team. Knowing that someone's profile is, for example, 'ENTP' does not provide other team members with sufficient information to remember how this information might differ from their own.

As team leader, knowing each member's profile and the strengths of their scoring can nevertheless be very useful in managing the team dynamic. For example, knowing your Is and your Es can be very important if you're trying to ensure that everyone contributes to a discussion. An extrovert is not necessarily being egotistical when they keep trying to dominate the conversation. It may be that they need to say ideas out loud before they can make sense of them. At the same time introverts can appear to have no interest in a discussion, but a common feature of introverted thinkers is that they like to contemplate what they want to say before speaking. Introverts also often prefer to be asked their opinion before they give it. Managing a discussion is therefore about keeping a balance between allowing the extroverts to think out loud, but then ensuring that introverts are also asked if they have anything to contribute.

You might want to consider which preferences are going to be more suited to managing complexity. Analytical Ts may be better at making the dispassionate decisions that are often required when you are in search of compromise. On the other hand, intuitive Ns may open up new ideas and possibilities. People with a strong *Judging* preference are going to be less comfortable with ambiguity and uncertainty than those with a high *Perceiving* score. There is probably no perfect set of preferences for a complex project. As discussed later in this section, the optimum profile is more likely to come from the collective diversity of the team.

PERSONALITY TRAITS

Another set of psychometric systems focus on personality *trait* rather than *type*. The best known are Hogan and NEO PI-R. A trait is a distinguishing quality or characteristic that we might ascribe to a person to reflect something that we see in them. From a psychological perspective, however, traits are the core descriptors around which patterns of behaviour are understood. Psychological Trait theory differs from Type theory in that it allows for behaviours to sit on a continuum between two extremes rather than putting individuals into a distinct category. There are hundreds of potential traits that have been identified, but there is an acceptance in occupational psychology circles that there are five 'super traits', which are often referred to as the Five Factors Model (FFM). These traits are summarised in Table 3.2.

Table 3.2 Five Factor Model (FFM) traits

Trait	Illustrative description
Neuroticism	The degree of emotional stability and the ability to manage emotions.
Extraversion	Outgoing and enthusiastic versus reserved and serious.
Openness	Imaginative and curious versus practical and traditional.
Agreeableness	Co-operative and friendly versus sceptical and direct.
Conscientiousness	Goal-focused and well organised versus easy-going and spontaneous.

The FFM is regarded as having a greater degree of scientific credibility than most other psychometric assessment systems in that it has been validated by four different research teams working independently. Researchers have been able to make a strong case for predicting an individual's success by combining certain traits when applied to specific roles. For example, individuals who show strong extroversion agreeableness and conscientious traits have been found to be more successful in the role of leader than those with lower scores. Similarly a person showing a strong conscientiousness trait will strive to deliver to high standards, but is likely to be more prone to stress if a lack of resources constrains their ability to perform. The real value of FFM assessments is in the high and low scores as they relate to each other. They have been shown to be a more reliable predictor of future behaviour than most other psychometric tests, particularly useful in anticipating performance under pressure.

There is a phenomenon called *leadership derailment,* which occurs when a person fails to meet the expectations made of them in a particular role for which they initially appeared to be well suited. When working within their normal capacity, performance can appear to be quite strong, but in a more pressurised environment they start to fail, causing significant collateral damage to their team and to their organisation in the process. Assessment tools based on the FFM can be useful in spotting the potential for derailment. Going into a difficult project, it might save the sponsors and the team a great deal of pain and uncertainty if key figures in the team are profiled on their resilience traits. This issue is covered in more detail in Chapter 6.

NEO and Hogan are relatively expensive to administer and time consuming to complete. Practitioners are required to demonstrate a level of competence in the field of psychology before they can undertake the training. Traits assessments tend to be used for senior-level recruitment rather than team building. In the future, as the FFM becomes better understood, it is likely that for high stakes projects, we will start to see an increase in the use of traits assessment.

MOTIVATIONAL VALUE SYSTEMS (MVS)

Another dimension to the field of psychological profiling is the Relationship Awareness theory developed by Dr Alias Porter in the 1970s. This theory is less concerned with a person's preferences and is more focused on the underlying motivations that drive behavioural choices. As Porter explained in a paper published in 1976:

> *Relationship Awareness Theory is based on the premise that one's behavior traits are consistent with what one finds gratifying in interpersonal relations and with concepts or beliefs one holds about how to interact with others to achieve those gratifications. Although many personality theories are about people, this theory was meant for people. It was intended to provide an effective means for understanding one's self and for understanding others so that interpersonal relationships could be mutually productive and gratifying. The theory was planned to help people organise their concepts of themselves and their concepts of others around three basic motivations: wanting to be of genuine help to others, wanting to be the leader of others, and wanting to be self-reliant and self-dependent.*

Porter created a psychometric assessment tool that he called the Strength Deployment Inventory or SDI. This system is popular as a team development tool as it is relatively easy to implement and remember. For all its simplicity, it offers a significant insight into our own motivational drivers and how they complement or contrast with others. The basic premise of Relationship Awareness theory is that our internal motivation fundamentally affects how we make sense of the world. To a greater or lesser extent, our behaviours are driven by a combination of three distinct MVS.

1. Altruistic–Nurturing MVS – concern for the protection, growth and welfare of others (Relationships).

2. Assertive–Directing MVS – concern for the organisation of time people and other resources to achieve desired results (Task completion).

3. Analytic–Autonomising MVS – concern for meaningful order being established and maintained (Process).

Responses to the SDI questionnaire provide a set of co-ordinates that are mapped onto a triangle as shown in Figure 3.1, allowing the individual to recognise the extent to which their motivational values are aligned to different behavioural drivers. As with the FFM, the profile of each individual is shown as a matter of degree. The closer one's co-ordinates are to one of the three corners, the stronger the motivational driver as compared to the other two. From a team perspective, it is therefore easy to create a team profile which shows how each person's motivation differs from the other members.

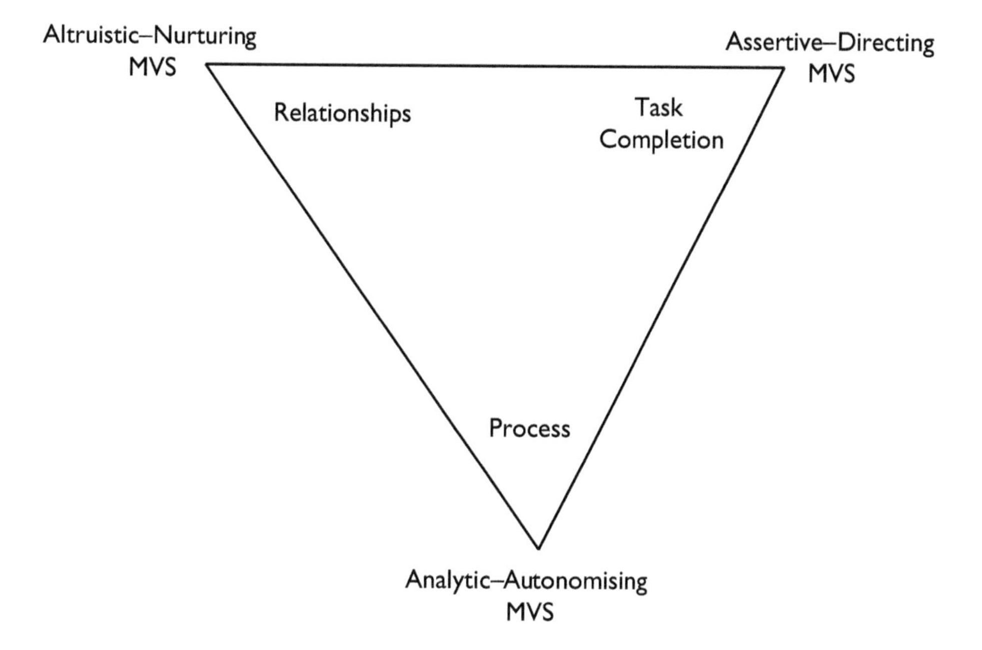

Figure 3.1 Illustration of the Strength Development Inventory (SDI) triangle

To illustrate my point about understanding differences, I will take the risk of providing a caricature of the profile of three typical team roles in a major project:

1. A designer with a strong Relationship MVS, who has a high degree of sensitivity to how others use and interact with the work that he has created.

2. A technical engineer with a strong Process MVS, who likes to work in a logical sequence, largely independent from the rest of the team.

3. A PM with a strong Task Completion MVS who approaches every problem in pragmatic way, and is highly motivated by task accomplishment.

Project meetings would be coloured by the features set out in Table 3.3.

Table 3.3 Illustration of character profiles based on different Motivational Value Systems (MVS)

Designer	Project Manager	Engineer
Likes to engage in conversations around different potential ideas.	Makes decisions quickly.	Likes to be certain before making decisions.
Values different ideas to see what might work.	Values efficiency and minimal waste of resources.	Values logic, precision and clarity.
Explains reasoning based around feelings.	Is in a hurry to get things done.	Expects others to be concerned with logic, details and matters of principle.
Likes to work in a harmonious environment with others.	Likes to lead.	Likes to be self-dependent.
Defines success as producing an elegant outcome.	Sees success as having hit a target.	Regards success as having used resources effectively.

The challenge for each of these characters is to understand that the differences in behaviours that they observe in the others are a function of the distinct way that each of them makes sense as to how the project should proceed.

The task-oriented PM wants to find the most efficient route, even if that means cutting corners. He is, therefore, often frustrated by the engineer who insists on following the rules. The designer gets upset when the PM appears to have no concern for the relationships between different members of the team, using language that he regards as lacking respect. Similarly, the engineer cannot comprehend why the designer has to talk so much before a decision is made. They all want the project to reach its goal, but each has a different perspective on how to get there.

THE VALUE OF PSYCHOMETRICS TO TEAM DEVELOPMENT

The information provided by psychometric tests can therefore be of a significant benefit to the project team coach. Hogan and NEO are potentially valuable when assembling a team. Being able to compare the personality traits of different candidates can provide some useful supplementary information when deciding who is going to fit into a critical role. It is worth noting, however, that such tests are not foolproof. Once someone understands how a questionnaire has been constructed, it is not difficult to adapt their responses to fit the profile that they think has been prescribed for the role.

Tools such as MBTI and SDI are cheaper and easier to implement as part of the team development process. When they are well facilitated, workshops designed to explore *preference* and *motivation* can be very effective in getting a new group to communicate at a more personal level. They can therefore be highly effective in starting the trust building process, and moving the group 'up the hill' towards becoming a real team.

Building a balanced team requires a mix of people who have different preferences, traits and motivations. A range of personalities will give you a wider base of perspective than a team in which most people think the same way. Diversity has the potential to not only enable the team to make better decisions but will also make it more resilient. To take advantage of diversity however, each member must be able to understand how their profiles vary so that they can make allowance for, and make good use of, the differences.

Psychometrics are therefore a worthwhile addition to the team coaching toolkit. They provide everyone on the team with a deeper level of personal information that helps improve communication and build trust. As team leader, they give you some information as to what sits below the surface. I would emphasise, however, that material that you get from these instruments should be treated as clues rather than evidence. It is important to remember that, in any given exchange, behaviour is heavily dominated by situation and context. It is best, therefore, to be aware of the temptation to limit your belief as to what your team members can achieve by presuming weaknesses that have not yet been proven.

The Influence of Culture

Another factor that creates invisible and potentially disruptive forces on a team is culture. This is an important phenomenon that is often ignored by PMs, even including those working in a cross-cultural environment. We are often aware that people in other countries, societies and even organisations have different beliefs and social rules, but then make no adjustment to our communication style when working with them. Culture is important to a project leader because it creates subtle forces that can support or impede how decisions affecting the project are made. Different cultures can also sometimes provide an explanation for behaviours that otherwise appear irrational and counter-productive. They can be observed at three distinct levels:

1. the macro or international level;
2. the organisational level;
3. the micro or sub-cultural level.

This section provides some short observations on each level.

Macro Cultural Influences

In an increasingly global market for project delivery, teams are assembled from an ever-widening skill base of different nationalities. The coaching philosophies discussed in the previous chapter of *first slowing down* and then *seeking to understand* are useful rules in thinking about how you might help a cross-cultural team to work together.

One of the most respected writers in this field, Geert Hofstede (2010) has created a useful entry point for a PM trying to understand how national cultures differ. Based on research that started in 1960s and then extended several times in subsequent decades, Hofstede's *Cultural Dimensions Theory* set out six indices against which different cultures can be assessed. A concise summary of each dimension is set out in Table 3.4.

Table 3.4 Hofstede's cultural dimensions framework

Index	Description
Power Distance index	A measure of the degree to which people lower down the hierarchy are prepared to accept that power is distributed unequally in their public, social and economic organisations.
Individualism versus Collectivism	The level of contrast between societies that appear to value personal achievement and independence as against family or tribal cultures where social cohesion and group loyalty are more important.
Uncertainty Avoidance index	A measurement of the level of tolerance society appears to have for uncertainty and the extent to which rules and systems are put in place to try to manage and constrain change.
Masculine versus Feminine	The predominance of male values such as competitiveness, ambition and power over cultures which place more importance on feminine values such as relationships and the quality of life.
Long-term versus Short-term Orientation	The level to which some societies focus on the future as contrasted with those that are concerned with living in the present and respecting the past.
Indulgence versus Restraint	The extent to which personal gratification is seen as something to be promoted and enjoyed, or constrained and regulated.

These six dimensions provide a broad agenda for potential discussion, although from a project delivery outcome some of the cultural indices may be more relevant than others. There is an obvious correlation with complexity and the extent to which some cultures are more adaptable to uncertainty than others. There are also some useful cultural pointers in recognising that decision making in a culture with a high *Power index* and a high *Collectivism* score are likely to be very different to those that are more *Consultative* and *Individual* oriented.

Once again, it is important to recognise that Hofstede's indices produce results that are generalisations, based on the aggregation of data. In a multicultural project team you are still dealing with people who will have different levels of belief in each of the attributes that are prescribed to their culture. These beliefs will also be tempered by their personal preferences, traits and motivations.

I was told the story of a team working on a very large transportation project, where the design team was effectively split between two groups, one based in Berlin and the other in London. My colleague was employed as a design manager with the remit of co-ordinating output of the two offices. He had anticipated that there would be a level of cultural clash but was surprised to see how well the groups worked together. His reflection was that both cities attract such a wide range of nationalities from around the world that the London office was not culturally British, nor the Berlin office culturally Germanic. Instead, he found that that the culture was much more focused on the delivery of the project design.

This story supports the outcome of a study done by Christopher Earley and Elaine Mosakowski (2000) into hybrid team cultures. They found that teams that are highly heterogeneous, that is, made up from a wide variety of cultural backgrounds, will initially struggle to work effectively together as they lack a common framework to understand each other. Over time, however, such teams develop their own particular organisational culture rather than adopting the culture of a parent organisation as is more commonly found in homogenous teams. The study concluded that given the right environmental conditions that allowed a team to work out its internal process, heterogeneous teams were frequently seen as more adept at creative problem solving than highly homogenous teams.

JOINT VENTURES

Interestingly the Earley and Masakowski study also observed that *partly heterogeneous* teams are often likely to struggle to perform effectively. This is because subgroups quickly appear as individuals align themselves to those with whom they feel a greater sense of affiliation. Under duress such teams quickly fall into a pattern of reduced communication and disengagement from the project. This is a common problem found in joint ventures where two or three organisations from different countries come together to deliver the project. The purpose in creating the joint venture may be to share risk or to extend the skill base. Multinational joint ventures often struggle because managers tasked with the delivery of the project underestimate the instinct for different nationalities to quickly form into separate tribes. Attempts in the start-up phase to establish working methodologies and processes struggle to make progress as each tribe fights to use the systems with which they are most familiar. The outcome of these early encounters is a bi or tri-national segmentation of the project where each sub-team focuses only on its own allotted task work. There is little collaboration, with the result that the project suffers from constant bickering as to who is responsible for any work that sits on the interface between the group's tasks. The same challenge also exists for joint ventures formed from businesses from the same country.

Organisational Cultures

At organisational level, cultures are usually more local. They may reflect the cultural influences of the country in which they are located, but at a managerial and operational level every organisation will have their own attitudes and beliefs that affect the way in which they work. Schein (2010) sees organisational culture is an abstract concept that can be used to explain various phenomena such as the tacit rules as to 'how things are done around here'. A project is effectively a temporary organisation. It pulls specialists together from a variety of sources, each of which will come to the table with their own cultural value systems. In teams formed from external consultants and contractors, it is easy to envisage that there will be differences in how they believe they should be representing their home organisations. Problems can be anticipated if their embedded value systems appear to clash. Quinn (1988) sets out a *competing values framework* that illustrates the potential for cultural discord. Figure 3.2 is an adapted version to illustrate my point.

A cultural clash differs from the personality clash in that it emerges from a difference in approach or belief rather than an emotional reaction driven by discomfort or subconscious fear. Looking at the model, one can see that a project sponsor such as a government department might have a dominant value system that seeks centralisation and control. A commercial contracting organisation on the other hand might have a strong bias towards productivity and profit generation. A third contrast might be a technology consultant whose organisational belief systems encourage creative insight and the development of individual thinking.

The three individuals from these organisations will each adopt a subtly different approach to the mechanisms that they use to deliver a project. In the early stages of the programme, such differences are unlikely to be particularly visible. They become much more important once the stresses on the project start to emerge. In some ways the different positions that arise from cultural differences can be the most difficult to reconcile. This is because it is hard for an individual to make a compromise that effectively separates her from the prevalent beliefs of her home organisation. The task is made easier if some form of discussion is had at the start of the project that brings cultural attitudes to the surface.

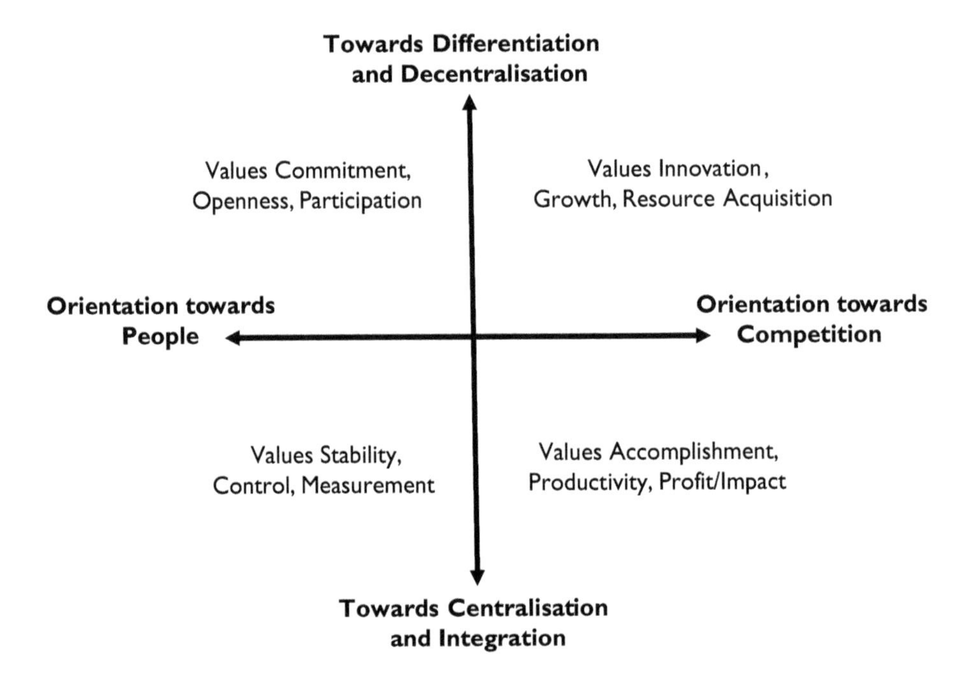

Figure 3.2 Competing values framework
Source: Adapted from Quinn (1988).

RECOGNISING SUBCULTURES

Teams that are formed from internal resources from *within* an organisation should not, on the face of it, have to manage the same challenges of competing values. In large organisations, however, the management challenge moves from the reconciliation of different organisational cultures to the problems created by internal subcultures. As Schein (2010, page 55) explains:

> *Much of what goes on inside an organisation that has existed for some time can best be understood as a set of interacting sub cultures operating within the larger context of the organisational culture. These subcultures share many of the assumptions of the total organisation but also hold assumptions beyond those of the total organisation usually reflecting their functional tasks, the occupations of their members, with their unique experiences.*

The larger the organisation, the more embedded and distinct these different cultures become. Schein observes that there are three generic subcultures in every private or public institution:

1. *The Operator subculture*: These are the teams who deliver what the organisation does. They make the products or deliver the services. They have a strong sense that they are the ones that make the business work. Their subculture is built upon the recognition of the need for human interaction and teamwork. They distrust process in so far as it lacks the flexibility to manage unexpected events.

2. *The Engineer subculture*: This is a subculture that emerges in teams who design the organisation's technological process and systems. Often coming from a technical background, they share similar educational and work experiences. The engineering mindset likes efficiency and tidiness, and the subculture therefore views people as a problem in that they are unpredictable. Where possible, they will try to design people out of the system.

3. *The Executive subculture*: Usually found in the senior management group whose perspective is shaped by the need to monitor and maintain the financial health of the organisation. The subculture is shaped by a sense of responsibility for the group's survival, combined with a low level of trust in the information that they receive from lower down the hierarchy.

Schien's point is that different subcultures will tend to look at the challenges facing the organisation from their own perspective. This is not a problem until the point that two teams decide on a path of action that is incompatible. This is an important issue for *internal* project teams. Recognising the different cultural perspectives of each team at the start of the project allows for a neutral discussion on the potential similarities and differences in values and beliefs. Left unacknowledged, any differences in cultural values will quickly come out at the first pressure point, but will appear as interpersonal differences rather than a much more significant challenge of a systemic clash.

CULTURAL WORKSHOPS

So how do you manage cultural difference? As mentioned earlier, trust is key to building a cohesive team, so your focus is around how the team members achieve some process gains early in the project cycle, whilst avoiding the potential for process loss. Frameworks such as those set out in Table 3.4 and Figure 3.2 are a useful mechanism for undertaking a preliminary review as to whether your team is likely to encounter a clash of cultural thinking or identity. The greater the potential damage, the more value there is in investing time and energy in an exercise that will reduce *cultural behavioural risk*. The concept that underpins such workshops is to get people talking about themselves in a neutral environment. The objective is to engage in open dialogue so that team members have the opportunity to explore for themselves the cultural differences that might exist at macro, organisational and subcultural levels. This requires some skilled facilitation, as we often do not necessarily recognise our own cultural beliefs until they are challenged by events.

One useful technique is to encourage team members to ask each other questions about the accuracy of their preconceptions. There is then an opportunity for either recognition that the perceptions are correct or that they need to be adjusted. The purpose is to create a sense of recognition that as far as the project outcome is concerned, one cultural approach is not better than another. The team need to understand that the prize for taking this exercise seriously is much greater cohesion and problem-solving capacity making the project experience far more fulfilling. By the same token, a failure to acknowledge cultural differences is likely to hold back the team's ability to work together when the project becomes more pressurised.

Marie's Story

When I was working in the Far East I organised several workshops with a hospitality group, two universities and professional designers/engineers to design the most innovative hotel bedroom. To do so, we ran a workshop in partnership with Dialogue in the Dark (DID), a social enterprise that seeks to raise awareness of the challenges faced by people with no sight or partially sighted. DID usually organises workshops in complete darkness for companies willing to improve communication within a team.

Using DID's methodology, we created an experience that required the participants (mainly architects, engineers and designers) to design a hotel bedroom. The twist was that the design process took place completely in the dark! Working with my team, DID's blind trainers, and thanks to a creative partnership with a perfumer, a material library and a soundscape artist, five groups of eight people were invited to open their senses and explore some unusual dimensions of space. They were given scents, material samples and had to listen to several bespoke music pieces. They were then asked to share with each other the images, colours and landscapes they could actually see, in spite of the dark. Based on their impressions and feelings, each group had to choose the samples they wanted to work with and had to work creatively together to develop a design concept for the hotel bedroom.

One of the fascinating outcomes that I noticed was that many of the restrictions of culture and hierarchy were forgotten as people were talking more freely and with respect and attention, one after the other, not in front of others, but with others, or for others. The darkness allowed them to express themselves with more confidence and space. In a culture which places great value on hierarchical respect it was surprising to hear the younger members of the groups articulating thoughts and feelings that would have remained unsaid in the light.

Another outcome was that after few minutes of physical adaptation in the dark, people loved being given the opportunity to reconnect with their senses, other than sight. They had to hold hands to walk to their seats and join their assigned group, and to touch each other when they had to give each other the scents and material samples around the table. This was unusual but it created an extraordinary feeling of connection, contact and solidarity.

Summary

This chapter has provided a brief initiation into the fascinating field of behavioural science. As an area of expertise it has been largely ignored by most professional bodies in their assessment criteria to attain qualified status. The dilemma is to decide how deeply into the subject a project management practitioner should go. After all, your job is to manage a project, not to become a therapist. My view is that even a small amount of knowledge as to what makes other people 'tick' is going to help you find a new level of understanding. If your role also fundamentally requires enabling people to work effectively together, then an extended knowledge of the factors that influence behaviours may well be a differentiator in your level of professional competence.

An essential module in learning to understand others is to recognise your own psychological filters. What are your particular traits and preferences? What motivates you to come to work and what drives you forward under pressure? Answering these questions is an exercise that you can do by yourself, but if you really want to understand 'your experience of your experience' it is worth seeking out a coach who can help you explore the different aspects of your personality. Having someone help you reflect and ask questions from a different perspective will help you make sense of your journey to this point in your career. The real value in this type of coaching exercise is that it can help reinforce your confidence in your particular strengths, whilst building an awareness of limitations that are created by your own particular blind spots.

PART II

A Model of Project Team Coaching

Behavioural models work best when they are applied to simple or simplistic situations. Models are a useful way of demonstrating the sequence, pattern or connection between different components of an ideal process. It is therefore, the nature of models to be general rather than specific and as such they are useful in providing perspective rather than prescribing a course of action. Complexity makes models less useful, in that it can be too difficult to map all of the competing and complementary forces that create a complex environment.

I have nevertheless created a model of project team coaching, which is illustrated in Figure PII.1. The purpose of the model is primarily to demonstrate a structure around which to connect the different interventions that are discussed on the second part of this book. The pyramid shape illustrates the layering effect of the different activities.

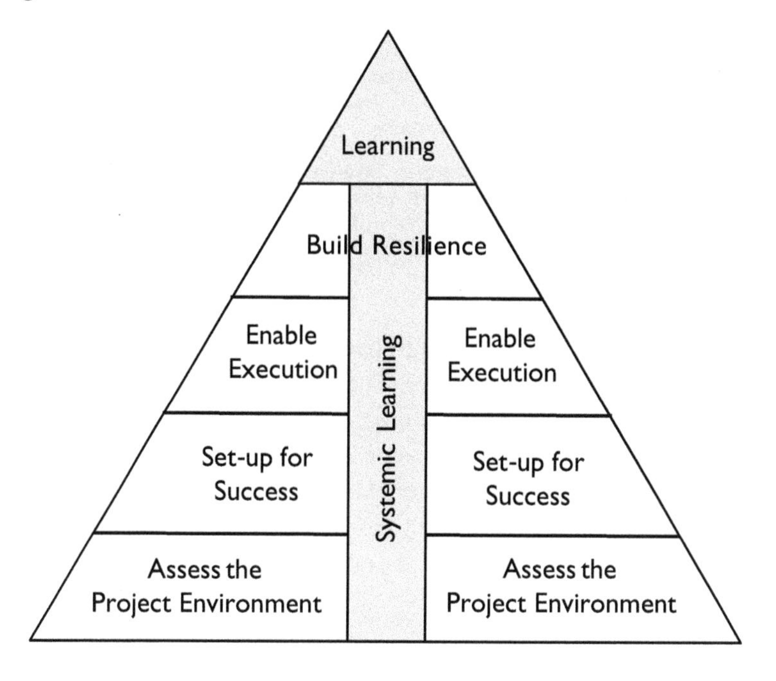

Figure PII.1 A model of project team coaching

A brief illustration of the content of each layer is set out in Table PII.1. I have chosen to use the term *layers* rather than levels as I wish to avoid the perception that project team coaching has to work to an inflexible structure or sequence. The term allows for the conceptual idea that each layer may be thick or thin, depending upon the circumstances of the project. As the following chapters elaborate, there are various techniques to help manage complexity. The layers of the pyramid therefore identify the different components that you might consider useful as you prepare for your next major assignment.

Table PII.1 The layers of team coaching

Layer	Description
Assess the systemic environment	Analysing the various factors that affect the project environment and engaging with the team and the sponsors to ensure that the project is adequately resourced. Check that all critical assumptions are valid rather than over optimistic.
Set up	The second base layer upon which the team is built. It is the point in the project where team coaching practices and interventions are going to have the greatest impact.
Enable execution	Once the project starts, the team coaching aspect of the role focuses on facilitating good behavioural process, primarily around interpersonal communication.
Build resilience	Helping the team withstand disruption and unexpected change. The coaching role also involves enabling the team to become comfortable with the uncertainty and ambiguity inherent in complex projects and programmes.
Learning	Ensuring that the team take time both during the project and at the end of each phase to learn from their experiences and to put that learning back into the project.

Part II of the book works through each layer and focuses on actions and ideas that can be applied in practice. The chapters are structured to shape a different way of thinking about how you might influence team behaviour, but the principal focus is on the practical application and approach of team coaching 'interventions'. It is not my intention, however, to be prescriptive. My hope is that you are encouraged to experiment with some of the ideas and learn from the experience. Over time you will then be able to build up your own model for coaching a project team.

Team Learning

Before we move into the content of the different layers it is first worth considering the topic of team learning. One of the primary roles of a coach working either with individuals or teams is to help them to *learn*. Coaching is not really about teaching in the context of passing on knowledge. It is more about facilitating a set of actions where people use their own thinking and experiences to turn new information into embedded knowledge. The model in Figure PII.1 shows *learning* as the top layer or capstone of the pyramid. This is potentially misleading as it implies that *team learning* is separate and distinct layer to the team coaching process. I have therefore shown learning as a systemic component that runs down through each of the other layers in the model. My objective is to illustrate that team learning should be a regular and distinctive exercise that is woven into the teams cycles of activity.

Undertaking a *lessons learned* exercise at the end of project, or even a project stage, is a part of the standard project management methodologies. The concept is supported by Hackman and Wageman (2005). They conclude that one of the important roles of a team coach is to help the team learning from the project experience at the end of the task cycle. They make the case that until the project is complete, all of the data required to carry out a review is not yet available. They also argue that whilst a group is focused on task completion, they are less likely to be able to reflect on what is happening.

The disadvantage of postponing any form of group learning until the end of the project is that the acquisition of new understanding comes too late to be of any value to the project. Complex projects are usually a new experience for most of the team members, requiring them to tackle problems that they have not encountered before. One of the core roles of a team coach is to turn individual experiences into 'group learning'. To be of any value, it must feed that learning back into the project so that the whole team increases its ability to manage the challenges of complexity.

If one were to look at the collection of individuals that make up the team, it is possible to see them as having a particular capacity of knowledge and experience that is available to deliver the start-up phase of the project. Capacity can be defined as 'the maximum amount that something can contain'. The great thing about human beings is that, unlike machines, our capacity for learning is not constrained by our physical environment and has the ability to expand as the project develops. The extent to which it actually grows will, however, depend upon the extent to which the team takes the time to engage in the process of collectively learning from each other's experiences. This expanded capacity is an (almost) free resource that the team can access as part of its mission. The only cost is the time required to pause and reflect.

I would therefore make the recommendation that a discussion on learning takes place early in the programme. Learning quickly from mistakes is invariably going to help improve future productivity. Similarly, acknowledging those activities that are working well helps reinforce good practices. There is, however, a deeper learning that comes from considering the systemic influences on the team, and the extent to which they may be creating obstacles to progress.

The Learning Cycle

If you have not come across concept before, it is useful to be aware of the implications of the adult learning cycle, which is based on the work of David Kolb (1984). The cycle is based around four distinct stages of activity as illustrated in Figure PII.2. Kolb's observation was that adults naturally join the cycle at different stages according to their particular preference. Hawkins (2011) picks up on the work of Honey and Mumford (1992) to illustrate the problems for teams that become stuck as a result of a tendency to try and short circuit the learning loop. For example, action-oriented teams will often get caught in the 'plan–action' cycle when new tactics are constantly being worked up to resolve particular problems but no new thinking emerges. The team therefore often struggles to make a significant leap forward. This is particularly a problem in industries with a strong transactional culture such as construction, where the project environment discourages the participants from taking time to review and reflect. Other teams can get stuck in an introspective loop where they reflect and plan, but are afraid to take the risk of trying their ideas out in practice.

For the team to embed their learning, they must make the investment required to work through all four stages of the cycle. This learning process takes time and practice, which can be difficult when the team are under pressure to be seen to be making progress. Putting a learning culture in place requires a leap of faith that you will achieve more in less time if you first slow down so that you can later speed up.

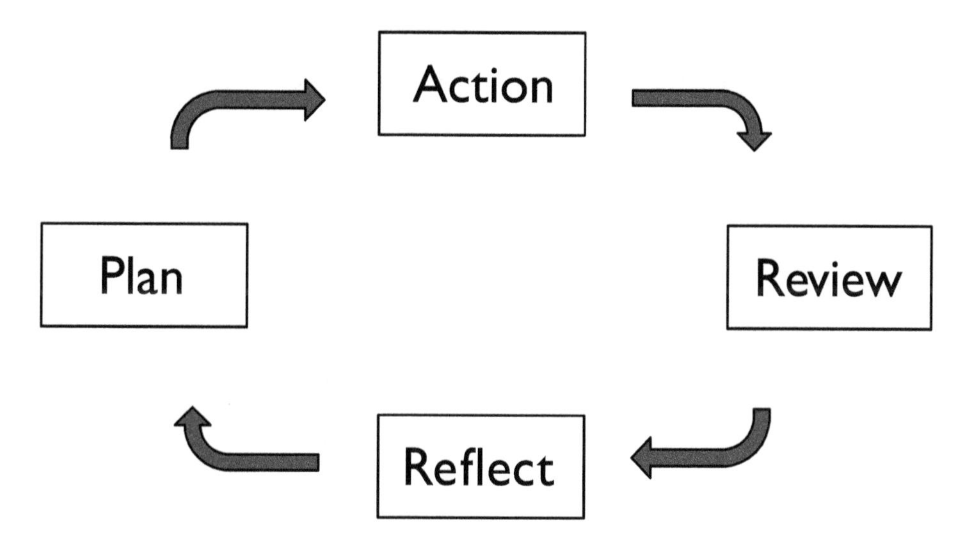

Figure PII.2 The learning cycle

You can probably find your own stories of projects where activity was confused with progress, only for the project to struggle to meet its targets. To tap into the resource of human ingenuity, one needs to create a team environment where individuals have the time to think as a group so that ideas and possibilities appear 'from the ether'. Creating a learning environment is the primary portal to access this resource. I have come across a number of different examples of doing this. Some teams set aside time to do 'lessons learned' exercises at the end of each phase of the project. Others factor in a learning review at the end of their monthly meeting. Perhaps the best examples come from those teams who habitually ask themselves the question, 'Why did that happen, what could be done differently and how do we avoid the same mistakes in the future?'

Unlearning

One of the less well-understood aspects of adult learning is the need to periodically *unlearn* knowledge from the past that is either now obsolete or is actually misleading. Unlearning is part of the process of making a paradigm shift, which recognises the constraints of transactional thinking and the options presented by collaborative engagement. In the same way that technology evolves, so should our internal processes around beliefs and assumptions. As the world around us changes we should logically adapt our ways of thinking to suit. Many people find this quite hard, until some form of crisis forces them into a re-evaluation. The tipping point comes when there is a realisation that the beliefs and behaviours that may have served you well on your journey to this point are now actually getting in the way. Unlearning is a state of mind rather than a process of deletion. It simply requires the recognition that a newer version of mental software is available which will help deal with tomorrow's challenges more effectively.

As a PM, this probably starts with your own need to unlearn some of the cornerstones of your working practices. What are the assumptions that may be limiting your ability to move beyond the transactional mindset?

Chapter 4
Building the Project Foundations

Layer One: Assess the Project Environment

Every project sits within a particular set of circumstances that could be described as the *systemic environment*. Some of these circumstances create the momentum for the project to move forward, whilst others will try to constrain it. These forces arise from a range of different factors, some of which are *macroeconomic* and others which are more local or *systemic*. Understanding these forces will help you assess how much preparation you need to do with the stakeholders before the project begins. Your *first* task as project coach should be to work with whatever members of your future team are available to understand the external factors that will have an impact on your ability to complete the project successfully.

MACROECONOMIC FACTORS

These are the 'big picture' issues that work at a regional, national or global level, and are largely out of the control of the sponsoring organisation. They can be identified using the classic PESTLE analysis tools that are a standard part most strategic planning exercises. The acronym stands for Political, Economic, Social, Technological, Legislative, Environmental. It is not my intention to explore these factors in any detail. The point is that a major project is nearly always initiated by change in one or more of these factors. It is therefore always worth understanding just what the macroeconomic drivers actually are. In the old economic model of the nineteenth and twentieth centuries, these factors tended to change slowly and to follow a pattern that was, to certain extent, predictable. In the twenty-first century, the rapid pace of change means that one can no longer assume that the PESTLE factors that were in place at the start on the project will not have shifted during the course of the programme. There is always the danger that a major adjustment may be introduced by events such as:

1. the loss of a key sponsor;
2. cancellation of funding;
3. legislative change;
4. cultural disapproval of the project process or outcomes;
5. the arrival of disruptive new technology.

Such events are difficult to predict but the signals of macroeconomic change are usually visible several months before they actually have an impact on the progress of the project. Project teams can often become so absorbed in the project that they lose touch with the changes that are going on in the outside world. Potential problems are ignored until the issues become critical, by which time it is more difficult to take evasive action. I am not arguing that you should develop a secondary qualification in economic theory but maintaining a degree of attention to the macroeconomic horizon and then facilitating a conversation about possible implications is a good habit to develop.

SYSTEMIC FACTORS

Systemic factors are those circumstances that *can* be directly influenced by the project sponsors and stakeholders. They are *systemic* in that they are based on organisational rather than personal drivers. These factors will differ with every project and so it is for the team to try and work out just what the critical variables might be. Every industry has its own particular culture, driven by a mixture of economics, experience and history. The construction of a large building will have a different team dynamic to a heavy engineering or a petrochemical project.

Certain factors affect most types of project but it is worth recognising that there is often a difference between the systemic factors that affect *internal* and *external* project environments. An *internal* project can be defined as one where the majority of time resource for the project is provided by individuals who are seconded, full or part time, from a role elsewhere the organisation. An *external* project will predominantly rely on a group of individuals selected from independent firms outside of the sponsoring organisation. The dynamics of these two types of teams will be quite different. Tables 4.2, 4.3 and 4.4 provide an illustration of the differences between project types, as well as those factors that will occur on both internal and external projects.

Table 4.1 Examples of systemic factors affecting external teams

Factor	Variable
Procurement method	Whether the team members were selected on the basis of the lowest tender, or negotiated as a preferred supplier.
Team familiarity	The extent to which team members have worked together before and have established working relationships.
Client experience	Where external teams are assembled, the sponsoring client will often have less experience in the project process than the technical specialists.
Organisational culture	The differences or similarities in values, norms and beliefs that individuals from different organisations use to identify their home team.
Project novelty	Has the team delivered this type of project before?

Table 4.2 Examples of systemic factors affecting internal teams

Factor	Variable
Resources availability	Getting people with the right skills allocated to the project.
Focus	Are the people seconded to the project on a full-time basis, or are they squeezing their contributions around their 'day job'?
Resource stability	Are the people allocated for the duration of the project or just a part?
Political influence	The tendency for individuals to compete with others in the team for wider political influence outside of the teams remit.
Siloed subcultures	Individuals allocated to the project from sub-groups which are out of alignment with the vision and purpose of the organisation.

Table 4.3 Examples of systemic factors affecting both internal and external teams

Factor	Variable
Team leadership	The systems are used to identify, commission and support the individual who will lead a project.
Sponsor engagement	The formal and informal styles of contact with the project sponsors.
Budget	The processes for creating approving and updating project budget.
Trust	The degree of control imposed on the team by the principle stakeholders.
Programme	The mechanisms used for imposing urgency on the team.

Table 4.4 Illustrations of paradoxes that can arise from the project environment

Objective		Constraint
Plan and think.	but	You must start immediately.
We want the best quality product.	but	We want the lowest price.
Keep everyone fully informed.	but	Maintain confidentiality.
Team needs to take pragmatic decisions to get the job done quickly.	but	Must also recognise the political processes and keep everybody happy.
Find the best people.	but	Every position needs to be tendered to the market.
Be innovative.	but	Minimise risk.
Everyone around the table should have an equal say in the decisions that we make.	but	The existing hierarchal authority must be respected.

Establishing an awareness of the team environment could be compared to a process of stabilising the ground upon which the project team will work. The firmer the footing, the quicker the team will find a stable basis for working together. If the ground is soft or uneven, there is a high chance that it will create problems for the team later on. As project leader you should be going into the project with 'your eyes wide open'. If some of the environmental factors look problematic, then you must acknowledge them to yourself and to the team. Don't make the common cognitive error of assuming that everything will probably be fine. As discussed in Chapter 1, our desire for a project to move forward often overrides our experience, causing us to ignore the early warning signals.

It is not unusual for a PM to find themself sitting in front of the project sponsor after the project has started, arguing that problems have occurred due to forces outside of the team's control. This is an uncomfortable discussion because our explanations now come across as excuses. It therefore makes sense to take a proactive approach to the potential challenge of a difficult project environment.

There is an exercise that I would advocate all PMs should use at the earliest possible stage of the project. The first step is to pick out roughly seven of the environmental factors that you believe could have an impact on the project. Draw them out in a continuum arrangement as illustrated in Figure 4.1. You can now rate each factor on a scale of one to ten, where one would have the most negative potential impact and ten the least. It is now very easy to come up with a number based on the combined scores for each variable. Numbers can be very meaningful, particularly for technical people.

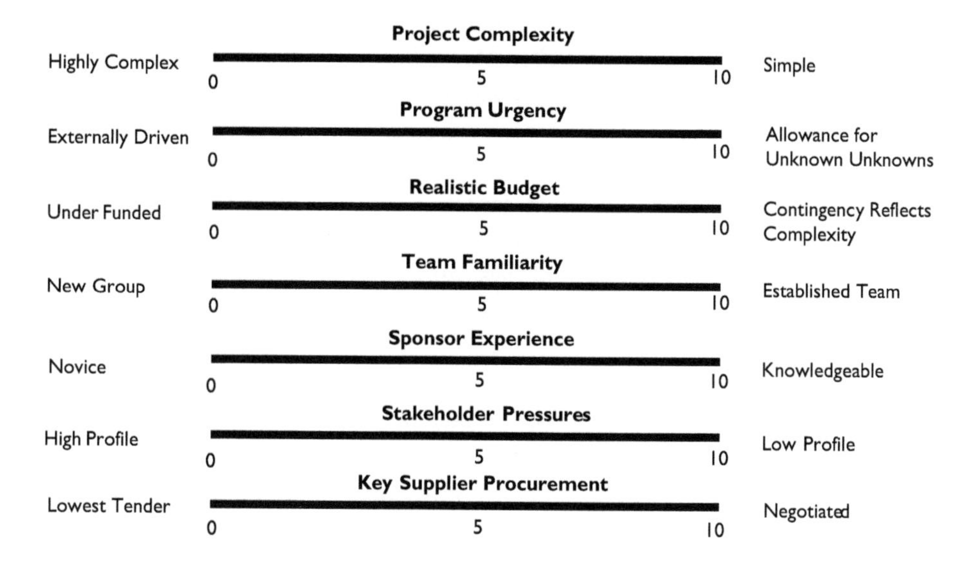

Figure 4.1 Framework for assessing the systemic environment

The real value of the process, however, is not the number, but the reasoning that each person doing the exercise can explain for arriving at their score. The coaching role within this exercise is to *create a discussion that requires the participants to think* about the impact of these factors in the future and to start to question their assumptions. If the environmental score is low, but the project is important, then everyone at least knows what they are signing up for. This is a great exercise to use with the project sponsor, particularly if they have limited experience of project delivery. It helps them identify gaps in their understanding as to how the project will work. It can also provide a neutral basis for arguing the case for adjustments to be made in those systemic factors that can be varied, such as resourcing of manpower, budgets or programme.

The coaching skill is to encourage a dialogue. Enabling people to engage in this type of conversation, ideally before resources are committed, allows the team and the sponsors to start a pattern of communication that will run throughout the project.

Cathy's Story

I have learned the hard way that you have to go into any big project with your eyes wide open. I remember one job where I was brought in as PM for an internal change programme. The 'client' was somebody from the finance team who had never done this type of project before. He was a bright young bloke, but he just assumed that if the Board had said it was going happen, then it would happen. It was really naive, and he completely failed to grasp the power of internal politics to make things difficult. The timescale was always going to be unrealistic, but the biggest problem was that we were reliant on a number of people being seconded from other parts of the organisation. These people for all meant to be working full time on the project but most of guys that turned up to the kick-off meeting were clearly only going to be able to work on this project in their spare time.

There were clearly some office politics going on as there were a few team members that just appeared to want to be awkward about everything. I could see from the start that this was not going to go well, but I just hoped that it would all somehow sort itself out. In hindsight I should have sat down with the finance guy at the very start and had a 'heart to heart' on why this project was heading for disaster. By the time we did have this conversation, the project was going seriously wrong. It was only when the Board realised that we were going to be three months late that things changed, and the Chief Exec got involved and suddenly everybody started behaving, but I don't think anyone came out of the project looking good.

THE MONEY NEEDS TO BE RIGHT

It is worth stating the obvious fact that if the money is not right then, one way or another, the project will fail. This may seem to be a statement of the blindingly obvious but a realistic assessment of the final cost is something that needs to be given a high priority in the early stages of the project. If the budget is insufficient, then the project will come under stress early in the programme, and will create strong dysfunctional forces within the team. Avoid complacency. The budget estimate should be challenged by a third party and a risk assessment carried out on the cost of the critical elements. High-risk items should be explored to confirm any assumptions before the project commences. Complex projects will always throw up problems that require additional resource, so it is essential that the team leader has some contingency sums available. I have come across numerous projects where the sponsor decided to remove any contingency from the budget in the belief that this would impose a degree of financial discipline on the team. This may be an effective mechanism in a transactional environment that is futile when faced with the unknown unknowns that arise in complex projects.

The *conspiracy of optimism* is a strong phenomenon. In hindsight, it is often easy to see that it was a mistake to push forward with a project that had little realistic chance of completion within the budget. It is worth recognising that our desire for activity often blinds us to the potential consequences of going into a commitment that will be financially disastrous for our business, and highly stressful to our team, our families and our body!

Managing Stakeholder Paradoxes

Managing complex projects, almost by definition, involves the need to manage the challenge of paradox. A paradox arises when someone makes a dual proposition that, when taken literally, is not possible to implement. Some examples are included in Table 4.4. Paradoxes often occur because the project environment creates a series of competing forces which require some form of trade off. The management of complexity requires acknowledging that, for the project to proceed there is very little that is black or white, just a series of different shades of grey. This ambiguity creates a challenge for a newly-formed team.

It is not simply about trying to design a solution that will suit the wants and needs of users within a limited budget. The task is to help identify, and make everyone aware of, the contradictions and inconsistencies that each stakeholder and team participant has within themselves as to what they expect the project to achieve. The most common response from team members, when faced with contradictory requirements, is to move to a position of safety and low risk. The result is a mismatch between the espoused team objectives and the reality of reduced output. Both stakeholders and team members need to recognise the risks inherent in these paradoxes and accept a degree of compromise. If the paradoxes arising from the project environment are not acknowledged, then as team leader you open yourself to a future problem. How do you demonstrate that the team is performing when it is not possible to satisfy both sets of demands?

Each large project will have its own paradoxes that arise from the personal and organisational aspirations of the key sponsors. The pattern in the examples set out in Table 4.4 is an illustration of a paradox created by a desire to be adventurous and innovative but at the same time minimise risk. Understanding and acknowledging these paradoxes gives the team a framework for discussing future problems, both amongst themselves and with the project stakeholders. Your task as leader is to ask the stakeholders to recognise the paradoxes in their requirements and help them articulate, not just their thoughts, but also their feelings. Often, however, our thoughts are difficult to articulate without appearing to choose one side or the other. It can therefore be very helpful to try and understand where the priorities really lie by mapping out where each person involved in the discussion feels they sit on the continuum. It is then possible to see that there is a point or a zone between the two extremes that indicates that there is a degree of bias towards one position or another. An example of a paradox chart is shown in Figure 4.2.

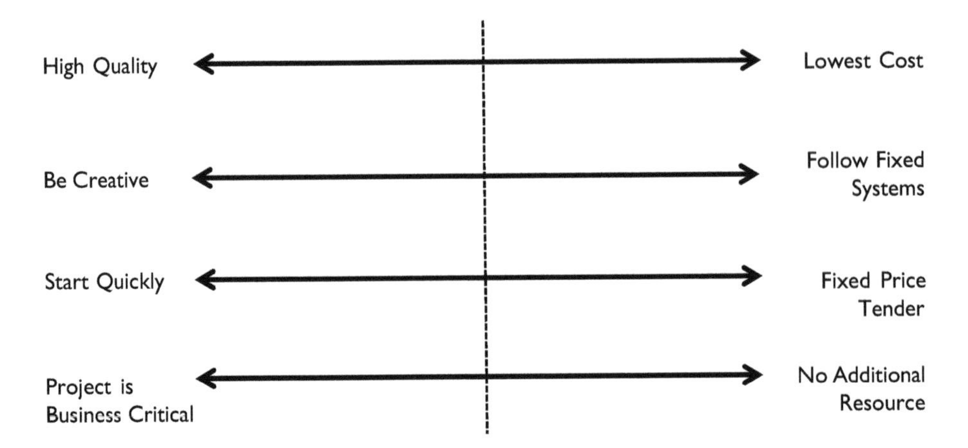

Figure 4.2 Example of a paradox chart

This exercise is well suited to a workshop format and should be seen as an important component of the project set up. The first step is to articulate the paradoxes that the team can see arising from the project. It is then a matter of asking a few of the stakeholders to explain their thinking as to why each extreme is important. Once the perimeters are clear, you can then invite each person in the room to mark on the chart where they feel comfortable on each particular paradox.

The coaching approach is to help the team first recognise their paradoxes and acknowledge that they exist. Some people are quite comfortable with ambiguity and can quickly come to terms with the trade offs required to find a solution. Technical people, however, tend to prefer certainty. The danger is that, in the absence of any recognition that the paradoxes exist, they will focus their assumptions on one end of the continuum. This is rarely a successful strategy as it requires completely ignoring any information which does not confirm the chosen viewpoint.

This exercise is similar to the process of assessing the project environment in that it also uses a continuum to facilitate a conversation. It differs, however, in that its purpose is to map where different stakeholder's priorities lie within each paradox. It also requires asking a different set of questions to a potentially wider stakeholder group. The output of this exercise is useful in that it:

- allows the individual to express their opinion without the need to explain exactly why;
- it reveals the collective average or zone with the majority are comfortable;
- it provides the team with a sense of where to pitch future decision making.

Layer Two: Project Set-up

Commencing a project with a coaching mindset starts with a series of interconnected processes that need to be implemented with belief and passion. The basic requirement is to set up a project so that the variables that impact upon the project environment are understood, and that everyone is starting from the same point. The project set-up forms the foundation upon which to find a degree of stability and consistency when the environmental conditions start to change.

In Chapter 1 we talked about the *conspiracy of optimism*, and the problems that are caused by making assumptions that turn out to be incorrect. This challenge is probably most acute just as the project is about to move from inception into the detailed planning phase. Before you set up a project, what assumptions are you making? One of the themes running through the stories that I have collected on unsuccessful projects was a misplaced optimism as to how the team members would interact. Four of the most common flawed assumptions were:

1. the client's behaviours will be consistent;
2. that everyone involved in the team will be committed to its success;
3. that everyone will behave in a rational and consistent manner even when under pressure;
4. that team members will support each other to get the job done.

The effect of these assumptions turning out to be incorrect was often cited as a primary contribution to the delay and cost overrun of a project. Most PMs have a good understanding of the concept of risk management and the development of risk registers to mitigate future disaster. My proposition is that you start every major project with the following set of assumptions:

- the client or project sponsor's behaviours are going to be erratic and changeable;
- that few of the team will be prepared to make any form of committment to the project;
- that, under pressure, the behaviour of a number of team members will regress to a transactional mindset;
- that team members can see no value in supporting their colleagues, even if it means they cannot perform their own roles effectively.

Given these assumptions, would you be inclined to put a bit of time and effort into some risk mitigation around behaviours? The remainder of this chapter is therefore devoted to the processes that, *when implemented effectively*, have a significant effect in improving team behaviours.

The textbooks on successful teams show a high degree of consensus on the critical stages of team set-up. The most common activities that are recommended are set out in Table 4.5.

Table 4.5 Typical components of a project set-up

Task	Objective
Team assembly	Get the right people on the bus.
Stakeholder management	Engage with all those individuals or groups who have an interest in the project.
Vision/Purpose	Establish a clear understanding in the team as to what is to be achieved, and why.
Roles and responsibilities	Clarity of who is accountable for doing what.
Team charter	Setting the ground rules as to how the team will behave when it is together, (and when it is apart).

These tasks are probably already in your existing start-up checklist. They consistently feature in the stories that I have collected on successful projects, which might be seen to reinforce their value. However, I also came across plenty of examples of *unsuccessful* projects where these set-up activities were also put in place. The difference was not in what was done, but critically *the extent to which the team members were engaged in the process.* I do not propose to rebuild the detailed arguments and references as to why each of these set-up components are important to a successful team, as they are covered fairly extensively in the literature on team performance. Instead, I want to focus on the need to rethink how these activities are undertaken, looking at the set-up process from a coaching perspective.

ASSESSMENT SCORING OF THE SET-UP PROCESS

My proposition is that the set-up phase of a complex project needs to be planned as a single exercise which has a number if integrated components. Let us assume that the project has been given the approval to proceed. You and your team are going to be assessed on how successfully the set-up part of the project is implemented. You will be assessed against the criteria that you feel is most relevant to the team's future success but your objective is to get as high a score as possible. The primary factor that will affect your ability to achieve a higher assessment will be the time and thought that you and the team are able to put into the planning and preparation of the different set-up activities that are described in the remainder of this chapter.

This is a different way of thinking about the project management process. It is diametrically opposed to the standard tick-in-the-box approach because you are focused *on the outcome of the set-up process* rather than on the application of the processes as an outcome in itself. This is important because the tasks are not necessarily sequential. As discussed later, some of the activities are iterative, in that they need to be revisited a number of times as new information or additional questions emerge.

John's Story

John is a senior manager in a large regulatory institution. Over the years he has worked for the organisation he has developed a reputation as a highly capable PM. A few years ago, John was asked to take on a critical project for the organisation. A decision had been made to split the regulatory body into two distinct entities, and legislation had been passed by Parliament setting the date when the formal separation of the institution would occur. The problem was that the existing systems of regulatory oversight were not set up to allow for easy division. The separation would require a complete rewrite of the rulebook.

The project had already gone through three false starts using the standard 'change by committee' approach. When John took on the challenge, the only fixed piece of information was the date that the new legislation required the separation to take place. He assembled a small internal team of people that he knew personally or who had a reputation as being highly competent in their areas of expertise.

The complexity in this project arose primarily because there was no template to follow. No one had done something like this to a regulatory body before. The changes would have significant implications for those businesses being subject to regulation, and would also create a period of uncertainty for every single member of staff within the organisation. This was therefore a high-stakes project!

The simplest approach would have been to work through the handbooks that set out how the regulatory process works. Stacked on top of each other, these books would have been over six-foot high. There simply wasn't time. The team would therefore have to work everything out from first principles. John put into place a process that had worked well for him before. Despite the pressure to take action, he took the time to set up all of the project systems before becoming immersed in the task of working through the detail. This included the following actions:

- finding a space for the team to work together;
- establishing how the team connections to the primary stakeholders would work;

- creating a process for constant feedback loops;
- taking time to make sure that each member of the team was clear on the scale of the challenge;
- agreeing with the team the processes that they would use to work together;
- agreeing who would be responsible for which aspects of the project.

As the projects got underway, the team were constantly updating their understanding of how to achieve the outcome. One of the most important team meetings was the 'wash up' session that was held every day at 6 o'clock in the evening. The purpose of the session was to refocus on the critical issues and who was dealing with them. From time to time, the Board sponsors would also attend this meeting, both to gauge the progress being made but also to give feedback to the team on issues where they were uncertain.

John describes himself as a project enabler rather than a PM. His method of working was to focus on the most complex issues facing the team at any one time and get them out of the way. He came to recognise early on in the project that to achieve the deadline each team member would have to find their own motivation to push themselves. From a management point of view, he therefore paid attention to each individual's hot buttons, encouraging them to choose which particular work streams they wished to take ownership of. He then focused on providing them with support rather than direction. He also tried to stay tuned to the mood in the room ensuring that small irritations didn't escalate into interpersonal issues.

The outcome was considered to be highly successful. Not only did the team work out a completely new set of procedures for the two new groups, but also managed to get all 3,000 members trained and ready by the separation date.

Gaining Commitment – Which Team are You On?

Before you get into the set-up phase it is a sensible idea to understand as much as you can about your team members and get a feel for the 'materials that you are working with'. As the team starts to assemble, some time should be spent on a one-to-one basis listening to them talk about the project and their ideas, hopes and aspirations. The majority of your prospective team members, whether they are an internal resource or external consultants, are likely to have a *home team*. This is the grouping in which they are formally employed, and where they have established relationships. This is also the group that will have the primary influence on issues such as remuneration and promotion. It would be normal, therefore, to expect the home team to have the strongest ties.

On a complex project, however, you need them to be on the *project team*. You are seeking their full engagement and commitment. If you don't manage to get this commitment, then you cannot rely on them to deliver what they promise when the pressure is on. So you need to do everything that you can to influence every member to make a *temporary switch of allegiance*.

You are looking for emotional commitment, not just cognitive engagement. You need the team members to care about the project and what it will achieve for the end users. You need to tap into the sources of energy that allow people to push themselves beyond the normal requirements of day-to-day work. To do this you must create an environment that will draw the team into the project, so that your project is far more interesting and enjoyable than anything else that they might be working on. You need to find out what motivates them.

Studies on motivation tell us that most people are motivated by:

- interesting work;
- stimulating colleagues;
- a degree of control of how they work;
- being part of a successful team;
- being part of delivering an inspiring vision.

The degree of interest, stimulation and control will, of course, vary between individuals. You are looking for the intrinsic motivators that are beyond making money for themselves or their firm. So you need to find out, one by one, what it is that gets them fired up and enthusiastic. It is a relatively simple procedure. You just *ask*, and then *really listen*.

Beware of those individuals whose motivation appears to be predominantly extrinsic. If their interest in the project appears to be focused on the short-term financial gain, then you are unlikely to find a great deal of loyalty to the team if a better opportunity to make money appears elsewhere. Money is a hygiene factor.

As discussed earlier, it needs to be right, but once it is settled, then most people will focus on those things that inspire or energise them.

Kevin's Story

Kevin is an experienced PM and cost manager working in the UK construction industry. He fondly remembers his involvement in the development of the American Air Museum at Duxford in Cambridge. The project started life in 1986 but it was ten years before the project was finally completed. Kevin remembers that the project had a particularly strong team ethos. It was held together by the client, who was the Director of the Imperial War Museum, and it was his passion for the project that proved to be a consistent source of inspiration, as funds were slowly being raised. The building is an adventurous design by Sir Norman Foster and Arup's Chris Wise. It features a curved concrete roof with a 90-metre open span. Given the time it took between initial concept and final completion, it would have been easy for the team to lose momentum. Kevin describes the team as being full of great people. They were a mixture of architects and engineers of a similar age, who all got on well together. They were tied together by a really strong desire for the project to happen, and so they quite often put more hours into the project than had originally been budgeted. This inevitably led to some difficult conversations with the managers in their home teams, but the sense of working together to create something unique was a very powerful motivating factor.

Once you feel that you have a better understanding as to what gets each team member fired up, you are in a position to start the set-up process. As previously discussed, this is not a linear progression. There are a number of headings or activities but, as illustrated in Figure 4.3, each one is interlinked with one or more of the others, and some of the exercises need to be completed in a number of stages. The set-up can start at any one of the steps identified, according to the situation that you find yourself in. The more important point is to maintain a focus on the overall impact of different tasks to get the team ready to move into action.

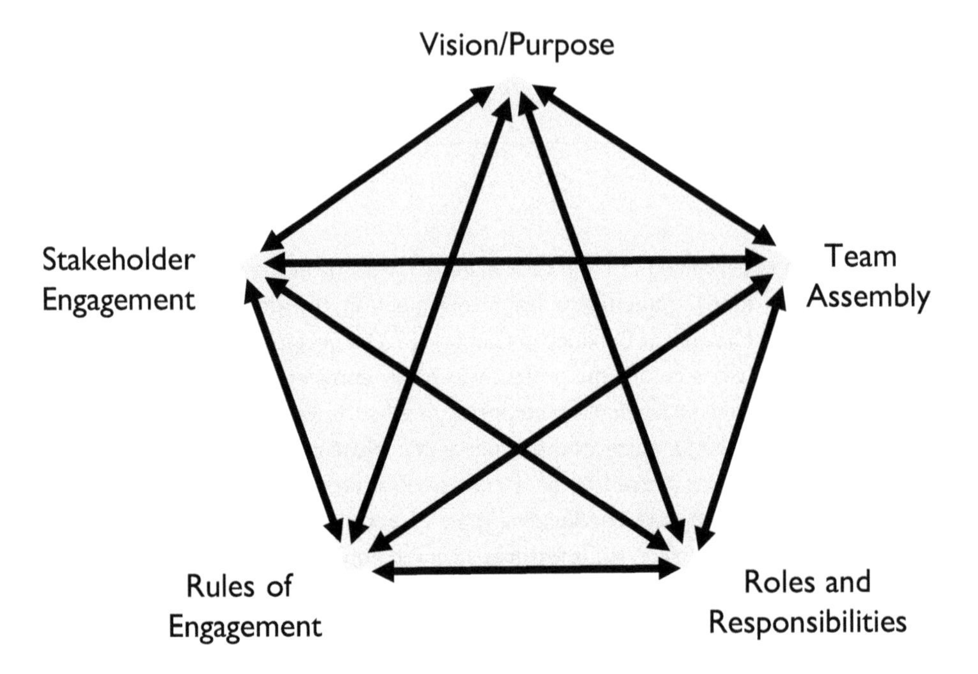

Figure 4.3 Interaction of team set-up activities

Team Assembly

As a PM you don't always get the opportunity to contribute to the decision into the people that are going to make up your team, but that is not an excuse not to try. Every textbook on team development places a strong emphasis on having the 'right people on the bus'. Teams often assemble slowly, over a period of time, as the project moves from concept development to feasibility and budget approval. Resource is allocated on an ad hoc basis until there is sufficient momentum, at which point a PM is brought on board. As one client explained to me, 'We rarely have a single point in time when the team comes together. It is a bit like a snowball rolling downhill, picking up whatever is in its path. Eventually we crash into a barrier and the PM has to reassemble the pieces.'

On major projects, where the participants are from externally appointed organisations, the tendering process can also distort the team leader's ability to find the right people. It is the nature of modern tendering procedures to encourage bid managers to exaggerate the skills and competencies of the individuals allocated to the project. Since bidding is an unpredictable method of building an order book, the same people will often be proposed for several projects at any one time. The outcome is that the winning bidder must enter into a fresh negotiation on the CVs being put forward. On transactional contracts, price tends to be more important than people, as the transactional mindset believes that people are an interchangeable resource. On complex projects, having the right mix of skills and attitudes makes the choice of key individuals much more important.

You may just be lucky and find that you have a set of people who just happen to interact in the way that you want. Far better, however, to remove this element of chance and whenever possible select the best people you can find. The golden rule of recruitment is to focus on behaviours and chemistry first, and then consider the depth of expertise that is required. The time devoted to recruitment will vary depending upon how much pressure you are under to get to project started. Assuming that you have the time and opportunity to influence the decision, the next consideration is around the dominant needs of your project. Is this a project that has a high level of technical uncertainty, or is good communication and engagement of a wider delivery group going to be more critical?

There are certain key roles that may be more important than others. One of the features of complex projects is a high level of uncertainty, so there are certain character traits that are going to be helpful. If you are going to use psychometrics to help make the choices, then use a trait assessment system discussed in Chapter 3, such as Hogan or NEO PI-R rather than MBTI. The three most useful traits of a complex project team are probably going to be openness, resilience and conscientiousness, but you also need to consider the benefit of having a mixture of profiles.

Unravelling complexity requires the team to have a collective problem-solving capacity, so diversity of personalities will be useful. There is a slight paradox here in that if the team is to be resilient under pressure, then it needs to gel together quickly. There is a subconscious tendency for us to form groups from people that we feel are similar to ourselves. So whilst interpersonal chemistry is important to quickly build up trust, the obvious danger is that if everyone on the team thinks the same way, this will lead to a much shallower pool of perspectives and potential solutions.

Clarity of Vision

Another really important component of the set-up is to find the *compulsive vision*. The team need to be as clear as possible, not just on *what* they are being asked to achieve but also *why* it is important. They need to know *for what purpose does this team exist*? On projects that are merely complicated, it should be relatively easy to identify what the outcome looks like, as there is a pattern of experiences that can be taken from the past and projected into the future. Complex projects can often be more difficult to visualise. The project sponsors may know the outcome they're seeking, but what it actually looks like, and how they are going to get there, are not clear at the start. The regulatory body in John's story (see above) that needed to be split into two distinct entities is a good example. The Board of directors understood the required outcome but just what the new arrangements would look like in terms of size, structure functionality and so on was not at all clear when the project was started.

It is therefore useful for the project team to work with the sponsors to take a blurry concept and build the different components of the picture so that a clearer vision of the future starts to emerge. This can be hard work and is inevitably time-consuming. The alternative, however, is to charge ahead, putting the preliminary tasks in place, anticipating that the project sponsor will eventually be able to provide a more detailed prescription and what they are seeking. More often than not, however, project teams are frustrated by a brief which is incomplete, contradictory and impractical.

This is partly because humans are generally not very good at looking into the future. We frequently struggle to articulate a clear vision of what we really want for the organisation we represent. Working out what we want takes time to formulate. As Hawkins (2011) points out, stakeholders are often better at explaining what they don't want than providing a concise and coherent articulation of just what they are seeking. They therefore often need help, and so it may require the team to keep going back and forth with different concepts until both parties have a clear picture what is needed.

In my research, I heard a number of experienced PMs talk about the need to be prepared to challenge the project sponsors, if they were getting mixed signals or ambiguous instructions. This is a lesson often learned the hard way, as there is an imbalance of power between the sponsor who is usually at a more senior level than the team. It is not easy to push back against the person who controls the money, but if you can establish an assertive pattern of communication early on in the project you will have a much better chance of managing everyone's expectations.

A clear vision can also be inspirational. This is not to be underestimated. Inspiration is one of the ultimate forms of influence as it stimulates positive emotions and can be highly motivating. It is, however, very personal.

You cannot set out to inspire, but you can do or say things that others will find inspirational. Stories are great ways of helping people find inspiration, as they stimulate the emotional connections that encourage people to take ownership of their own opportunities and challenges.

Rob's Story

Rob tells a story about the design of the technical research centre for a Formula 1 team. 'They had assembled a team of external consultants to design the facility, but the project was also going to involve a lot of internal people as well. With their expertise in motor sport, they understood the necessity of having a *real team* deliver the project as opposed to a *work group*. So the managing director called together every member of the team who would have a role in the project, from the lead architect through to the lowest grade of technician. From memory there were 60 or 70 of us in the room. He sat on a stool at the front of a lecture theatre and said, "I am just going to spend five minutes explaining to you what I think this project is going to achieve." Sixty minutes later everybody in the room was going, "Yes okay we get it, we understand, we know where you are coming from, we want to be part of this." I suppose a part of it was the glamour of the name, of it being Formula 1, but it was also his vision, and where he wanted to go. It just inspired us. One hour of his time put the whole team in the right direction. We then spent the day doing team building and workshops with different members of different organisations to help build the relationships, but it was his one hour of vision that got us focused.'

The project vision is a concise summary of the commissioning parties' objectives and the outcome. It is that they want to see when the project is completed. Coaching techniques based around the process of enquiry can help stakeholders work out what shape the future might be, and allows the exploration of alternative options. These alternatives need to be spoken out loud, as only then can a clearer image start to form. This needs to be a patient process, where the sponsors are encouraged to explore possibilities rather than an exchange of views as to why a proposal is unlikely to work. It goes back the rule of influence whereby you *seek first to understand, and then be understood.*

Stakeholder Engagement

Much of the research into team performance shows a high correlation between project success and stakeholder engagement. It is not surprising therefore that managing stakeholder relationships is a standard part of the project management checklist. And yet, lack of engagement is regularly reported as one of the most common areas of client dissatisfaction. The transactional mindset regards the engagement process as a task to be completed. The coaching approach is to focus on gaining alignment of all the parties connected with the projects towards a common vision. The authors of the RICS guidance note (2014) on the subject recognise that stakeholder engagement is a 'non-technical capability' that involves:

- juggling a mix of technical, financial and human challenges simultaneously;
- influencing others and balancing conflicting stakeholder interests;
- communicating effectively;
- applying intuition, emotional intelligence and empathy;
- building relationships and maintaining trust;
- dealing with ambiguity, uncertainty, risk and unknown unknowns;
- working over long timescales and with evolving objectives, constraints and environments.

As discussed in Chapter 1, these are not the typical skills required in the early stages of a PM's career. They do, however, sit comfortably with a coaching style of leadership, where your concern is to first understand, and then decide your strategies for influence.

The problem with communication is the huge amount of time and energy required to do it well. Organisations have a limited amount of resource to spend on communicating with stakeholders, so it is worthwhile thinking through where it is best directed. On complex projects, there are some stakeholder groups where engagement is critical. These are the people with a high level of interest in the project, as well as the power to influence what resources are made available. These critical stakeholders come from four distinct groups (see Table 4.6).

Table 4.6 Critical stakeholder groups

Stakeholder	Influence	Perspective	Principle concern
Sponsor/Budget Holder	Has control of the allocation of resources.	Strategic	What will the project achieve for the organisation?
Project Instigator	Commissions the project and assembles resources.	Process	Is the correct process being adopted?
Power User	Specifies the desired outcome.	Function	Will the project enable us to do fulfil our role?
Concerned Outsider	Can exercise wider political or economic influence on the sponsor.	Environment	How will this project affect our community?

Each of these individuals or groups will have a different perspective as to how the project should proceed, and the extent to which they wish to be involved. The process of engagement becomes difficult when each of the four groups regards themselves as the principal stakeholder, particularly if they have different priorities which may be in direct competition with each other. In some major institutions, such as government departments or large universities, each of these groups have further subgroups adding more diversity to the challenge of engagement and communication. Add in the forces of economic and political change and one can imagine a degree of complication that is potentially overwhelming. In such circumstances, it is tempting to stop trying to manage stakeholder relationships and instead simply react to requests for information on a casual basis.

Nick's Story

A PM working in the energy industry told me a story of a project with a large utility company who needed to upgrade a major operational facility. The project was commissioned by the companies' executive Board but implementation was passed to the firm's Facilities Management (FM) team, as there was no other in-house capability for managing major projects. The FM team were capable of managing their existing portfolio of properties, but were out of their depth when dealing with the range of decisions that were needed to tender a major project in the market. The PM recognised that, as a matter of pride, the facilities guys wanted to retain ownership of the project, even if they lacked the skills and the resource. Attempting to step in and take control would have been resisted and put a strain on the relationship.

The challenge was therefore to work through an iterative exploration of the environmental factors affecting the project so that the FM team were eventually able to specify the work packages. The project team could then start the design tasks for which they had been commissioned. This initial exercise was outside of the scope of works that the PM had anticipated, and even involved seconding staff to work with the FM team to build the necessary data sets. The outcome however was very successful, as the process helped generate a high degree of trust between the client and the delivery team, which allowed the project to proceed at a fast pace once it got underway.

Setting the Ground Rules

Do you know what sort of behavioural norms you would like to see established within the project team? As discussed earlier, as the project leader you have a limited number of opportunities to shape team behaviours. The primary opportunity is at the start, when the rest of the team is still trying to work out the social rules of the group. You could direct the group by setting out how you expect everyone to comply with a set of rules that you believe should govern the team's behaviours. The problem in relying on a directional style is that you have no sense as to whether the group agrees with you or not. The survival instinct when faced with a highly directive leader is to nod in agreement and keep your thoughts to yourself. Humans have a strong tendency to try and undermine any laws that are imposed on them, but will usually comply and reinforce rules that they feel that they created. Your objective, therefore, is to enable a discussion on how the team should work together and allow the co-creation of a set of rules of engagement that will guide team behaviours.

TEAM CHARTERS

It has become increasingly fashionable to set up a team charter at the start of the project. There is a degree of disparity of opinion as to just what the purpose of the charter actually is, and what it should include. Some PMs believe that the charter should set out the goals and objectives of the team, summarising the contract between the project sponsors and the participants. Others feel it should simply focus on team behaviours and output. The idea of assessing the framework within which the project team will operate has a lot to recommend it. In my research, however, I found many examples where the team charter was treated as a tick-in-the-box process and was often seen as counter-productive. The problem occurs when team charters become a paper-based exercise which is perceived as hollow. For example, I came across a technical contractor who produced a document at one of the early project meetings which he explained was a standard team charter which was used on all of their projects. In reality, the document set out an aspirational schedule of service standards, espousing a range of laudable collaborative behaviours. Whilst the sentiment behind this type of document may have been sincere, there was no ownership by any member of the project team of the prescribed commitments. Sure enough, when the pressure on the project increased, the contractor reverted to transactional behaviours and the charter was consequently irrelevant.

The team coaching methodology is to draw out the views and opinions of others so that each member hears what has been said, and is then able to decide upon how the social norms of the group will work. One of the most effective ways of building a set of behavioural rules is to use the team's previous experiences, as reflected in their stories.

USING STORIES TO CREATE THE GROUND RULES

Stories are a great mechanism for human beings to communicate with each other. They are a highly effective mechanism for explaining our desires and aspirations, without the need to elaborate or justify. When people tell their stories we are often drawn in and find our own meaning from them. We tend to listen to stories and engage with them at a much deeper level than if someone was trying to explain a theory or an idea. Stories are therefore really useful as a mechanism to co-create your team's rules of engagement.

The process works by asking each member of the team to briefly tell the story of one of the best projects in which they have been involved, and to explain why. Similarly, they should then tell the story of one of the worst project experiences and reflect on the cause of failure. It is important to start with a positive event, as there is a danger that the conversation otherwise becomes stuck in a negative groove. Each story will be different but themes will start to emerge that you can map out. It is important to have a mix of both positive and negative experiences, as it is the counterpoints that reinforce the messages. Do not be tempted to allow the session to appear to focus primarily on one particular aspect of the teamwork. It is also important to be vague to what the story should be about. If you instruct the group to talk about projects around a specific area then you may constrain the range of observations and experiences that are available to the team as a whole.

In my experience, the stories will start to build a series of contrasting themes so that one person might describe a project that was well set up, whilst another may talk about the situation where everyone was in too much of a hurry to start. The stories may throw up one or two ideas or areas for concern that you may not have previously considered. Many of the themes will nevertheless be familiar to you, as most projects suffer from similar ailments caused by poor interpersonal understanding. The point about the stories, however, is that they bring the issues to life and connect with the team at an emotional level. Once everyone has had a chance to speak, you can then pick out the key themes from each story. The team will then be ready to draft their *rules of engagement.* You can ask the team to agree which features and behaviours from the positive list they want to apply to this project. You can also highlight behaviours that the group agrees should not be tolerated. At the end of the exercise everyone should feel that they have participated in the creation of the ground rules. They are therefore much more likely to adopt them.

The context for any team setting up their rules of engagement is to remember that the purpose is not to regulate behaviours when conditions are benign, but to enable the team to work effectively together when the pressure is on. The meeting agenda therefore needs to consider issues such as:

- giving and receiving feedback;
- mechanisms for conflict resolution;
- protocols for debate and dialogue;
- good and bad meeting behaviours.

Producing a written document is to a certain extent optional. If all of the team members were part of the development of the rules of engagement, then they will remember them. Documentation is therefore of more value when introducing new members into the team as part of their 'induction'.

Accountability – Setting the Performance Bar

The set-up phase of the project is the time that each member of the team enters into a contract to deliver their part in the project. This is not simply about the paper document that deals with the transactional exchange of services and cash. On a complex project, if the project is correctly established, such contracts will be seen to be a superficial arrangement that has limited impact on what actually happens when the project gets underway. The real contract is deeper. It is the process of establishing mutual comprehension and obtaining personal commitment. It is the phase where the members move from being a *work group* to a team, or not, as the case may be.

The initial component of this contract is the establishment of clear roles and responsibilities. The exercise requires the group to articulate to each other just what they think they are going to be required to do. This may need to be a more prescriptive process for some teams than it is for others. In teams formed from external contractors, each one has been engaged to provide specific services. They joined the team with a reasonably clear idea of what their own contribution should be, and what they think they're going to be accountable for. Internal teams differ in that they are usually assembled from resources made available by different parts of the organisation. Each member may have been chosen as the representative of their organisational function, for example, finance, engineering, marketing and so on. Alternatively they may have been selected on the basis of their aptitude for the anticipated tasks, or simply their availability. Members of internal teams may therefore often be less clear as to their prospective role and what the team is going to expect of them.

ROLE CLARITY AND TASK AMBIGUITY

Whilst everyone on the team should be clear with each other as to what they can be expected to deliver, there will inevitably be times when gaps appear that were not anticipated once the project gets underway. One of the features of my collection of stories on strong team performance was the apparent willingness of various team members to step in and take on work that was not envisaged as part of their agreed role. A PM gave me a great example:

> *There are always gaps that you cannot plan for and you just have to do the best you can. When the team is working well together, I find people quite often stepping in to help when they don't necessarily have to. It just seems to be the natural thing to do if you want to get the project to work. I remember once working with an architect who lent his drafting technicians to the structural engineer for a weekend, to make sure they got the engineering drawings out for the following Monday. It was the only way we were going to keep ahead off a very demanding programme.*

Gratton and Erikson (2007) pick up on the desirability of getting some clarity on a role whilst being more ambiguous as to the tasks that are attached to it.

Setting out who is responsible for delivering certain outputs early in the project avoids the need for continual negotiation around turf issues. On the other hand, the advantage of being less specific as to who owns certain tasks allows a team to work out for themselves how to address a problem. Clarifying responsibilities is important because it 'sets the bar' for those parts of the project that each member is prepared to hold themselves accountable to deliver. There are two forms of accountability within a team:

1. Formal – the contractually specified need to fulfil the obligations set out in a legal document.

2. Informal – the emotionally driven need to fulfil the moral or personal commitments made to one's peers.

As we have established, one of the features of complexity is the high chance of change as the team create new information, and plans are then adjusted. Formal accountability is only effective for as long as the activities specified in the contract remain unchanged. As soon as the needs of the project environment shifts, such documents become a much weaker basis for demanding performance.

Accountability works at both an individual level and a mutual level. Individual accountability relates to those aspects of performance for which each team member takes ownership. Mutual accountability occurs only when the group recognise that they have a collective obligation to deliver. Katzenback and Smith (1993, page 60) state that:

> *at its core team accountability is about the sincere promises we make to ourselves and others, promises that underpin two critical aspects of teams: commitment and trust. By promising to hold ourselves accountable to the team's goals, we each earn the right to express our views about all aspects of the team's effort and to have our views receive a fair and constructive hearing. By following through on such a promise, we preserve and extend the trust upon which any team must be built.*

Establishing mutual accountability is a significant step up from a collection of individuals assembled as a *work group*, and cannot be assumed to occur as a natural development. Many teams never achieve the position where each member feels they have the right to challenge other members regarding their actions or behaviours. This issue is covered in more detail in Chapter 6, so, for now, I just want to make the point that establishing the basis for accountability must be done at the start. If the issue is left open, then once the project gets underway, each member will have to make their own assumptions at their level of individual accountability, and the chances of successfully holding each other to account without creating friction in the team is very low.

Why Do Teams Fail to Plan?

None of the ideas or processes set out in this chapter are conceptually complicated. Nor are they difficult to implement. Most people are aware of the old adage that if you fail to plan then you are planning to fail. And yet there are so many examples of disastrous projects where the lack of effective project set-up was identified as one of the root causes of failure. The different reasons offered by my interviewees will probably have a ring of familiarity:

COMPLACENCY

The project team believe that they know that they are technically competent and have no need to work through the set-up process. One story given to me featured a number of very experienced professionals who were being quite obstructive in a set-up workshop. When challenged, they claimed that they had worked on enough projects over their career to know what they were doing. They therefore felt that the workshop was a waste of time. Buckling under the pressure, the client instructed the facilitator to shorten the session. Within two months however, relationships in the project team started to unravel as issues arose that could easily have been resolved at the start, but had now caused these same professionals to stop talking to each other.

IMPATIENCE

There are nearly always substantial pressures on a project team to start as soon as possible. If a project has an outcome for which there is a compulsive need, the sooner that need is fulfilled, the sooner the sponsoring organisation can proceed with its mission. There is consequently a strong desire to compress the programme, irrespective of the technical and logistical realities.

INEXPERIENCE

Both sponsor and the project team assume that transactional methodologies will be sufficient even though the project shows all of the indicators of complexity.

LACK OF CONSULTATION

In my research I came across a number of stories where the project team were presented with a programme that had already been agreed between the project sponsor and stakeholders without any consultation with the project team. The deadline was already impossible to achieve and so there was strong pressure to make an immediate start, with the hope that things would turn out for the best. Sadly, this was not often the case.

LACK OF BUDGET

A common complaint amongst the PMs that I interviewed was that their clients were simply not prepared to pay for the cost of running team-building workshops. This is perhaps the poorest excuse for not putting in place proper set-up procedures. In their defence, many project sponsors have limited experience of project implementation. They often need help in raising their awareness of the factors that influence project success and project failure. In the context of the overall budget for the project, the cost of facilitated workshops is nominal, particularly if one considers the total cost of project failure.

Summary

There is a philosophical dimension to project set-up. Do you believe the future is something that happens to you, or do you believe that you have the opportunity to shape your own destiny? For some people, taking time to get the behaviours and team processes in place is a matter of risk management and mitigation. For others, it is a part of the creative process, or a component of the overall investment strategy.

The end of the set-up process is the start of the beginning of the project. If you have managed to align the mindset of the project sponsor and the team members successfully, everyone now knows what needs doing, how it will be done, and most of importantly of all, why it needs doing. As the project environment starts to shift, and the forces of complexity start to create uncertainty, good set-up will keep the team on track and increase its resilience under pressure.

Chapter 5
Working With the Team through Project Execution

Layer Three: Enabling Execution

Moving into the execution phase of the project cycle, the team can finally get on with the tasks that they have been commissioned to perform. The coaching aspect of the PM's role becomes less active, and the leadership needs of the team become a priority. Your coaching responsibilities have not however been discharged. The processes and behavioural norms that the team should have established during the set-up phase must now be reinforced and embedded. As I have tried to emphasise at different points in this book, positive team dynamics are a direct function of interpersonal trust. Team coaching is a process aimed at both building trust and maintaining it. The good work achieved in your set-up phase can quickly become undone by a few careless comments or an ill-considered email.

The coaching role now shifts from proactive influencer to a more passive function as the custodian of the teams newly established values and behavioural standards. That part of your mind that maintains an awareness of the team as a distinct entity should continually be observing the team's different interactions and asking the question, 'Who or what is creating process gain in our output, and where are the dysfunctional forces that might get in the way in the future?'

This chapter covers a number of observations from the literature on group dynamics on the factors that will enable you to influence the team's interactions though their meetings and their communication strategies.

ADOPTING A DUAL PERSPECTIVE

The leader/coach mindset requires developing a dual perspective. When the team is in execution mode you may need to immerse yourself in the project and when necessary lead from the front. At other times, the team needs support from behind. Understanding just what support is needed requires taking a systemic viewpoint. The starting position is to see the team as an entity itself, rather than a collection of individuals. The team is therefore a system that will develop its own specific behavioural norms. As discussed in Chapter 2, a team also operates within a series of wider systems that make up its external environment, which will influence the behaviours of the individual members. This might seem an esoteric observation but it serves to make the point that to understand what is happening in the team, you need to see past the actions of the individual and put them in the context of the different systems in which they specifically operate.

Project teams are temporary organisations. They start with a 'family' of a few members and can then grow substantially as the project progresses. A project is an organic system, whose dynamics will be influenced by the systems from which it has evolved, but will nevertheless establish its own behavioural norms. Over time, the group will develop tacit rules that will guide what is said, what is not said, what issues are dealt with and what is ignored. When you are sitting in the centre of a group, you are inevitably also contributing to these invisible behavioural forces. They develop over time as a reaction to surrounding events and so as the team leader you may not notice them. As team coach, however, you should try to periodically take a 'bird's eye view' of the team and again ask yourself that question, 'So what is going on here?'

The Dynamics of Communication

It is worth taking a step back and analysing the communication process. In its simplest form the sender has information that she wishes to pass on in the form of sound, words, body language or other actions. The receiver takes in the signals as raw data, which he then interprets with his own filters as information. The receiver can then decide what to do with that information in terms of whether it is useful and trustworthy, or should be disregarded. The purpose of this simplistic analysis is to make the point that just because we tell someone something, it does not mean that they have understood it in the same way. As discussed in earlier sections, everyone has different filters through which they take data and then make sense of it. It is a form of *interference* that can distort the data and create scope for miscommunication by the sender and misinterpretation by the receiver. This interference becomes greater over distance and over time. Your role as team coach is to try and spot where interference may be creating problems, and take whatever steps are appropriate to promote clarity.

Miscommunication and misinterpretation are part of the human condition and are, therefore, to a degree, inevitable. These factors nevertheless have the potential to quickly derail a team's ability to develop trust and initiate a regression into transactional behaviours. It is therefore helpful to establish a communication strategy that sets the context, both for intergroup and interpersonal relationships. Human beings have a unique capacity to make meaning of the actions and words of others. If we do not understand them then we work hard to fill in the gaps. Our starting point in making sense of some new information is the context in which we understand the message to have been sent. If we believe that the sender has a positive intent then we are more likely to form a positive perspective. If, on the other hand, our filters perceive that the sender is being ambiguous or defensive, we will quickly form a negative opinion.

You will not really know how a group of people will work together until they start to interact with each other. An aspirational team coaching skill is to be able to recognise the pattern of the interactions between different team members. The interpersonal dynamics that are important are those that have a degree of repetition, where the same behaviours can be noticed in different scenarios or situations. In stable conditions, professional etiquette anticipates that most people will interact politely, at least in the early stages when the team are getting to know one another. As time progresses, you are more likely to observe minor disputes and disagreements that do not necessarily correlate with the behavioural norms of the team. At a superficial level, it is easy to dismiss such disputes as a difference of personality. Real team dynamics are much more subtle as they are a reflection of our unconscious internal drivers.

A useful explanation of meeting behaviours is provided by David Kantor (2012). His research into dynamic communication shows that there is a structure to all human exchange. We rarely notice these structures as we are usually too focused on the content and style of the conversation. For those interested in learning more about conversational dynamics, Kantor sets out four levels of communication structure that an observer can look for to understand how to 'read the room'.

LEVEL 1 – ACTION STANCES

When you know what you are looking for, it is possible to recognise the different speech patterns that identify a *Move* to initiate action, or an *Oppose* to block a Move. Other patterns include a *Follow* which supports a Move or an Oppose, and a *Bystand*, which often attempts to reconcile competing actions.

Recognising these patterns of verbal exchange is useful if you notice that something is not working well in your team meetings and you are not sure why. For example, when a conversation starts to follow a *Move–Oppose* pattern between two individuals irrespective of the topic, you should start looking for clues in the next level of dynamics.

LEVEL 2 – COMMUNICATION DOMAINS

These are the personal influences that arise from our individual psychological drivers. How someone emphasises a particular message will depend upon whether the communication comes from their primary concern for *Affect* (feeling), *Power* (completion/achievement/influence) or *Meaning* (new ideas, or ways of understanding). Where the individuals involved have a strong affiliation for one of these domains there is likely to be a significant gap in mutual comprehension of the others perspective. The communication domains are a reflection of internal motivation, and so there is a correlation with the psychometric profiles discussed in Chapter 3.

LEVEL 3 – OPERATING SYSTEMS

Communication styles will vary according to whether the individuals are used to operating in *Open, Closed* or *Random* operating systems. These operating systems reflect the culture of the participant's organisation, and the way that they are used to sharing information. *Closed* cultures are usually strongly hierarchical where tacit rules dictate when and how conversations should play out. *Open* systems tend to focus on processes that try to achieve consensus and commitment, where the orientation is to encourage full participation. By contrast, *Random* systems are more comfortable with individual views that do not conform to any conventional model. Their intention is to encourage creativity and exploration of ideas. Kantor emphasises that one system is not necessarily better than any of the others as each have distinct benefits, but also has the potential to create dysfunctional relationships.

For internal teams operating within *Open* or *Closed* systems, there is a danger that they become stuck in negative feedback loops caused by the rules which govern how information is exchanged. For external teams where individuals come from cultures that employ different communication systems, there is obvious scope for misunderstanding arising from the clash of style.

LEVEL 4 – CHILDHOOD STORIES

The impact of the events from childhood, which become shaped into stories around which we create our identity. This is moving into deeper psychological territory and it is a space that the team coach might choose not to explore. It is nevertheless important to recognise that when the group is under pressure, the behavioural dynamics that emerge are primarily influenced by each person's childhood experiences.

This brief summary of Kantor's work is not an attempt to create a shortcut in developing the skills to be required to analyse patterns of conversation. My purpose is to make you aware that there are analytical processes that can be used to encourage the team to develop collaborative communication habits.

Paul's Story

This project turned out okay in the end, but it required a lot of heavy lifting. It was a project in the Netherlands for a large pharmaceutical company. It needed to work to a very tight timeframe and it had a multitude of stakeholders. We spent a lot of time trying to find common ground between them. We were just about to start when, despite an agreement on a common approach, the main stakeholder decided to change his requirements. So we ended up with a solution that negated all previous negotiations and provided one principle solution that compromised many of the others.

The project only survived because of the collaborative relationship that had developed between three individuals. The key relationships were with the PM, the client's representative who was from the HR team and with myself leading the design team. We managed to pull the project out of the mud largely thanks to the HR representative. She knew her way through all of the politics of the organisation and had a feel for where the problems might arise. She spent a lot of time making the social investment in calling and emailing the PM and myself in the good times when the project was in steady-state, before everything crashed. So she built a high degree of confidence between us at an early stage when everything was still going fine. This meant that we could trust what she was telling us, and encouraged us to be open and honest with her. I think that her integrity transmitted through to the other stakeholders so that in the end the project was seen to have achieved a satisfactory outcome.

DIRECT, FORMAL AND INFORMAL COMMUNICATION

The patterns for communication are established during the set-up process where systems, procedures and behavioural protocols all contribute to the communication framework. For example, a clear *vision* for the project creates the context for all project communications, the *rules of engagement* set the tone and frequency, and the *roles and responsibilities* establish the map of who is expected to say what. As mentioned earlier, however, it is not the processes that make a difference but how the team uses them. Communications cannot become a pattern until there has been a degree of repetition. This brings us to the idea of using different communication channels.

Communication can occur through a variety of different routes, some of which are more effective than others. Peter Robertson (2005) identifies three distinct communication channels. These are *direct* or face-to-face, *formal* (written) and *informal* (spoken). Communication structures within teams tend to be set out by levels of line authority, that is, from senior managers to junior staff. The structures are important when using direct communication as they add credibility, the implication being that the message is supported by the senior people in the organisation.

Direct, or face-to-face communications are regarded as having the highest level of potential impact as they are a formal statement of 'reality' at a particular moment in time. Being face-to-face, they also have the ability to include non-verbal signals such as body language, tone and context, which add considerably to the perception of authenticity. Direct communications also give the receiver the opportunity to ask for clarification in the moment and therefore reduce the potential for distortion.

Formal communication is usually issued in the form of a written document. As a mechanism for transmitting a message it works best when used as a support for face-to-face communication. It is less effective as a primary channel in that formal communication will often struggle to clearly articulate the implications of complexity. The receivers of written documents will often try and fill in the gaps for themselves, creating scope for ambiguity and misinterpretation. The use of neutral language is therefore important in written communication, particularly when using a medium such as email. The problem with neutral language is that it loses its capacity to stimulate an emotional response. The flip side however is the amazing capacity for human beings to take offence from carelessly drafted wording.

Informal communication can often be the most influential, and also the most mis-directive of the three channels. We tend to use informal communication when there is uncertainty or inconsistency in the formal messages being transmitted. As we try to fill in the gaps, we seek out conversations with others who may be impacted by change or uncertainty. We place a high degree of credibility on what is often viewed as 'gossip', particularly when this unofficial information can either provide us with a degree of comfort, or confirm our suspicions.

To establish a pattern requires frequency and consistency. Frequency is about timing and setting an expectation as to when formal or direct communication events are likely to occur. This might range from a weekly progress meeting involving all of the team, to a periodic session to reconnect with the project stakeholders. Frequency also comes from the output from such events and how notes and minutes are written and distributed.

Information is most effectively received when the data transmitted through each of the three channels is consistent, and the messages reinforce each other. The pattern that one is seeking comes from a style and approach that encourages the receiver to take the messages at face value, without the need for further confirmation from other sources. From a behavioural perspective, messages need to have a high degree authenticity and credibility. These are two of the primary attributes that build trust. In contrast, there are two bad communication habits that will destroy trust very quickly:

1. Avoid ambiguity in your own messages.
   It's really important to recognise that in a challenging project environment, any message which is ambiguous will be interpreted as having a negative implication. This is because our psychological filters are more tuned to identify threats than they are to perceive opportunities. If there are any gaps in the information provided, and then we will fill them in with our own data to create a message that warns us to anticipate danger. As Robinson (2005, page 141) points out, 'people do not react to direct danger, but rather to the statistical degree of danger that increases as more unknown factors enter the environment.' The communication challenge is therefore to seen to be as open and as clear as makes sense at any particular stage in the project.

2. Don't confuse information with power.
   A common theme from my collection of stories was the recurring tale of the PM who was perceived by the team to be holding back information, and keeping them disconnected from the project sponsor. Each story has its own particular circumstance, but the outcome in each story was a distrust in the motives of the PM leading to a low level of commitment from the other members of the team. It was not the lack of information that created the frustration and anxiety but the sense that the team members were being purposefully put into a position where they were not in control of their ability to do their work. The idea that information is a source of power comes from a transactional mindset. The assumption that 'I will have more control over you if I hold back information' is flawed in itself, but on a complex project is potentially disastrous.

This is not just a task for the project leader. Your objective should be to coach the team to adopt a pattern of communication that is congruent with the values and mission of the project. When the project environment is regularly shifting, it becomes essential that everyone on the team has the same information and is able to apply a similar meaning as to its implications.

My final point on communication patterns is to remember not to confuse frequency of events with communication impact. Simply because the team meets for a regular weekly meeting does not mean that you have established an effective pattern of communication. It is not the event but how it is structured and managed that will dictate whether the team's communication culture creates synergies or is merely a forum for reinforcing discontent. This brings us to the important topic of meetings.

Managing Meetings

As PM your role is often to lead the many meetings that are the team's primary form of collective engagement. From a coaching perspective, however, team meetings are the place where collaborative behaviours are shaped and embedded. It is therefore worth taking a step back from time to time and thinking about how effective your meetings are in managing a complex environment. The set-up phase will have required a number of different types of meeting, from one-to-one engagements through to off-site workshops. As the project progresses into the delivery phase, there is a danger that meetings fall into an ineffective routine.

Getting the right people around a table to focus on the right issues gives everyone the chance to exchange information, clarify its meaning and agree a course of action. Project meetings should energise, not stupefy. They are, after all, the time when the team get to share their experiences and find solutions that enable progress. Your team should leave every project meeting with a clear idea of their next actions, and a reminder of the shared vision and mission as to why they are part of the project.

Each team develops its own meeting culture, according to the environmental circumstances of the project. Internal teams will have a different meeting culture to External teams. In order to provide a degree of insight into how you might improve your teams project meetings. I have summarised the thoughts of my interviewees, as well as some other published commentators on the secret of having a good meeting.

1. THE RIGHT TYPE OF MEETING

Perhaps the biggest mistake that most team leaders make is to try and cram as much as possible into the one weekly or monthly team meeting. Everyone involved in the project is then invited to turn up whether the agenda is relevant to their role or not. Patrick Lencioni (2002) uses the term 'meeting stew' to describe the tendency to try and cover every type of issue that needs to be discussed in the same meeting. He presents a coherent argument for distinguishing the different types of meetings that a team should have according to the varying types of discussion that is required.

Once the project is running, the critical resource to be managed is the time of the project team members. It should not be wasted and so, from a coaching standpoint, the need is to think systemically and set up the meeting structures to optimise the interactions that the project requires. Table 5.1 sets out some of the alternative types of meetings one would expect to find on a major project. As can be seen, each type of meeting has a different nature, and may often only require the presence of part of the team. The output and the time required for each meeting type will also vary.

Table 5.1 Illustration of the nature of different meeting types

Meeting type	Typical agenda	Nature of the meeting	Output
Progress	An update of progress to date and any additional matters of concern.	Regular, short and precise.	Concise minutes.
Problem solving	Collective engagement on a problem that impacts on the progress of the project.	Creative. Should include members of the team who can offer different insights.	Clear decision and then action.
Strategic	Big picture items, such as how to approach potential challenges from a changing environment.	Periodic. Exploratory.	Adjusted project execution plan.
Learning	What is working and what needs to change.	Reflective.	Written summary and agreement to change.
Technical	Discussion on integration of team member's individual tasks with other members.	Ad hoc. Should not involve the whole team.	Technical progression or escalation.

2. SET THE RIGHT AGENDA

Using the *analysis of meeting type* not only helps to make sure that time is well used, but also informs the shape of the agenda for each type of meeting. Experience indicates that it is important not to overfill the agenda. The biggest issues should be at or near the top. They are the items that require the participants' attention and energy. You should anticipate that the items lower down the agenda will tend to get rushed so be careful to allocate time where it is needed. It is often useful to start with the bigger picture to remind the participants of the context for the discussion before moving into the detail. It is my personal opinion that it is probably not a great strategy to start a project meeting with a review of financial data. Whilst numbers are required to be able to assess certain aspects of progress, they are usually retrospective and rarely inspire or energise.

3. INVITE THE RIGHT PEOPLE

Another advantage of recognising different meeting types is that it enables you to get the right people to attend. Time is often wasted when decisions are postponed because information is lacking or further approval is required.

Another form of analysis that may be helpful in setting your meeting strategy is to understand the differing roles that may be required.

3. *The Primary Participant* – typically a major influencer in the group. They need to be fully engaged throughout the meeting. Their input is essential.

4. *The Specialist* – their role is to provide information to the team on specific technical issues. They rarely need to attend the whole session but, if they remain, their role should switch to that of *Observer*.

5. *The Observer* – they are there to understand what is happening in the project but do not anticipate making an active contribution to the discussion. Their reason for attending is primarily to collect information, so their contribution should generally be around questions and clarifications. This is not to belittle their value to the meeting and it is important to that they should be encouraged to speak if they have a point that will help improve the quality of the discussion. Research is clear that 'sideways' perspectives are a great way of helping a team avoid the tendency towards 'groupthink'.

6. *The Representative* – their primary purpose is to take care of the particular interests of their department or tribe. They typically offer a one-sided perspective. Their views should be acknowledged, but should not be allowed to derail or dominate the discussion.

The problem in many meetings is that these roles can become confused, allowing too many voices speaking at cross purposes. When dealing with complex matters, it can be useful to try and distinguish the roles required for each issue. For example, the attendance of *Observers* and *Representatives* should be restricted to *Progress* meetings, except where the agenda addresses their specific issues, in which case their role should shift to being a *Primary Participant.*

Jim's Story

This was a project up on the northern border of the United States where we were establishing a new mine. I came into the project some time after it had started. Setting up a mine in a remote location requires a lot of different specialist skills, but it gets much more complicated in a harsh physical environment. The project had already had two separate PMs who had struggled to get the site properly established. Both had tried to impose an autocratic style, which just didn't work. I think that there were just too many interfaces for anyone with a need for 'control' to handle. Four of us were sent up there to form the new management team for the project, and although we hadn't worked together before we just seemed to click very quickly. We each recognised the need to establish a collaborative team culture, and so we agreed that time needed to be invested to set the project up in the right way.

Keeping the local community on side was always going to be critical to the mine's long-term success, so we instigated a series of workshops to get all of the stakeholders engaged in what we were trying to do. We made sure that we kept the communication loop open so that we were continually checking that they were happy with our approach. This made things much easier as the project progressed. We also spent time pausing to work out a clear sense of mission as to what we were trying to achieve. We then did our best to make sure that everyone involved in the project 'got it'.

There were so many different activities going on over such a large site that we decided to hold weekly progress meetings for all our staff at 8.30 every Tuesday morning. All work stopped for an hour so that everyone, from the senior PMs through to the admin staff, could get up to speed on what was happening. We worked around a rough agenda that changed depending upon what needed to be communicated. We would start off with those things that were going well and then talk about what was behind schedule. Some of the external contractors were often bemused by this meeting, seeing it as taking time away from productive activity. The feedback from our staff however was really positive. I think the key was that the senior managers were always involved and so the session was never seen as an artificial exercise. As time went on we started to get some really good suggestions coming in from the staff, which I think illustrated how well the communication plan was working. I think that these sessions also helped created a strong sense that we were all one team.

We eventually brought the project in on budget and ahead of schedule. I'm an engineer by training and definitely a 'type A' personality (organised, driven, impatient), so I have never thought of myself as being particularly people-oriented. On this project, however, it was as if all of my experience came together and I was able to put in place all those lessons I have learned in the past. It was probably one of the highlights of my career.

4. THE OPTIMUM NUMBER OF PARTICIPANTS

Meeting numbers are not critical for progress meetings, where the primary purpose is to provide update information but not to discuss or debate its implications. However, where there is a need for the team to find a collective solution to an issue or to make a decision based on judgement then it becomes much more cumbersome if there are too many people around the table. There is no scientific evidence to establish how many people should attend a *discussion*, but there appears to be a degree of consensus that the optimum number is somewhere between five and eight participants. Beyond this number, the dynamics of the group will shift. Up to eight people, and the meeting can usually engage all those present. If there are more than eight, a number of attendees will sit back and let the most dominant characters do most of the interaction. If you are not sure about this phenomenon, then observe what happens the next time you are part of a group where membership shifts between six to ten members.

5. PARTICIPATION – BEING PRESENT

Where you are running *Problem-solving, Strategic* or *Learning* meetings, you need everyone to be engaged in taking in new information and contributing to the discussion. You want everyone to be 'present', that is, they are in your meeting, focused on your agenda and are not drifting off into issues that are outside of the meeting. People get bored if they are not engaged. You can see it in their body language and where their eyes are focused. It becomes much more obvious when someone is continuously looking at their smartphone. The extent to which you establish the right meeting culture for your team will depend on the ground rules established by the team in the set-up phase, and the extent to which they are enforced in the early days of the team's first few meetings. So what are your team's agreed rules on the most common disruptive behaviours listed below?

- turning up late to the meeting;
- interrupting when someone else is speaking;
- taking the discussion off into a personal agenda;
- leaving early without giving notice;

- starting a meeting by opening up their computer and logging onto the WiFi system;
- constantly checking email on a smartphone or tablet;
- openly responding to emails during the meeting;
- bringing papers into the meeting that are not part of the agenda;
- leaving the meeting before a discussion has been concluded.

Bad meeting behaviours tend to be subconsciously subversive, rather than intentionally disruptive. A team may start with the best intentions, but if these activities are seen as being acceptable then they will become established as a default and will become an increasing obstacle to the team's effectiveness as the project progresses. Such behaviours are common in teams that are heading towards dysfunction, and are an indication that the members may have lost their sense of engagement with the project.

6. CREATIVE TENSION: DISCUSSING THE UNDISCUSSABLES

Lencioni (2002) believes that a good meeting has to have an element of drama. He advocates the need for the leader of the meeting to unearth areas of disagreement and nudge the participants to voice differing opinions. He believes that it is critical that the leader sets out an expectation that there will need to be a debate, and that it will initially feel uncomfortable, particularly for those team members who are not used to confrontation. The ability to challenge each other's thinking is however an important component developing resilience in the team, as will be discussed in the next chapter.

Facilitation Skills

Another key skill for the project coach is facilitation. There are times when you need the group to engage in a broader-based discussion than can be achieved in a typical project meeting. This is when the workshop format can be very useful as a mechanism to get a greater level of contribution from every member of the team. Workshops can be time-consuming and are often seen by project sponsors as a luxury. Yet there is probably no other comparable mechanism for enabling a new team to get to know each other, or for an established team to find new ways of thinking about old problems.

The success of a workshop depends very much on the skill of the individual who is facilitating the session.

An important attribute of the facilitator role is to have a neutral position within the team, so that you can lead the discussion without being perceived to have a personal agenda. As project leader, you are quite likely to have strong and often passionate views on a particular issue. It is therefore sometimes difficult to lead the discussion from a neutral starting point. For this reason, you may need to find an independent facilitator to run the session. There are often occasions, however, when an issue needs to be 'work shopped' without the time to arrange a separate session. If you have learned to shift towards a coaching style, taking on the facilitation role will seem natural to the team.

The mechanics of the facilitation process will vary depending upon what the group needs to think about. As illustrated in Table 5.2, one can see that a different approach will be needed depending upon the issue that needs to be worked through.

Table 5.2 Facilitation scenarios

Issue requirement	Description	The facilitator's objective
Exploration	A creative session that will identify a range of potential solutions.	Create an environment where the team feels expansive and open to alternatives. Identify and remove barriers to creative thinking.
Examination	A technical session that seeks to test the viability of a solution.	Keep the team focused on facts, and questioning assumptions.
Arbitration	A session that seeks to settle differences of opinion as to the solution proposed.	Find points of agreement and then build compromise.
Reconciliation	A session designed to restore working relationships on a project that has started to fail.	Uncover systemic causes and encourage acknowledgement of contribution to problem.

I see the main purpose of workshops as being to draw out as many different views as possible. Whatever the issue under discussion, there should be a common starting assumption amongst each member that no one person has all of the information required to reach a decision. Roger Schwarz (2002, page 332) explains that:

> *people have to believe that you are genuinely as interested in understanding their point of view as you are in having them understand yours. This means holding the core assumption that you have some of the information, others have additional information and each of you may be missing things that the others can see.*

I have facilitated many sessions with groups and teams, both as a manager and as a consultant. I have also taken part in sessions that were brilliantly facilitated by others. You will have your own experiences to call upon and there is plenty of material published on the subject. If I were to pick out some of the main features of a good facilitation practice, I would include the following:

SET-UP

Think about how many people are going to be in the room and how they need to connect and communicate with each other. How are you going to set the seating plan, whether it is *boardroom, horse shoe* or *conference* style? You also need to consider how information is going to be presented and recorded and the availability of flipcharts, whiteboards, projections screens and so on.

NO PASSENGERS

It should be an established principle that everyone is expected to contribute. Recognise that it is easier for people to speak in a room, once they have spoken. This is the reason why most facilitators use some form of icebreaker to start the session. Make sure that this initial session does not eat into the time needed to get through the agenda. In my experience the best introductory sessions are over within 15 minutes irrespective of the size of the group. Some people love to talk, whilst others prefer to be invited to speak. As the facilitator you should try to ensure that in the first main session of the morning, every person in the room is seen to have provided some input into the discussion.

DON'T CROWD THE AGENDA

It is tempting to use the time when the team are together to squeeze a number of subsidiary issues onto the agenda. This should be resisted, as the point about a workshop is to provide time to talk and explore around important issues. I have found it useful to work to the principle of having one primary theme based around three key questions. This structure helps the team focus on its business and should allow for deeper consideration of the problem.

MAINTAIN ENERGY

Keep the room moving. Avoid having everyone remain seated for more than an hour. Use flipcharts and whiteboards to encourage them to move into different positions and to interact in different ways. Keep breaking the team into different subgroups.

STICK TO YOUR VALUES

The ground rules used in a workshop should be the same as those agreed by the team in their initial rules of engagement, for example, open discussion, timekeeping, no blame culture and so on. If non-team members attend the workshop then it is a good idea to bring them up to speed as to how the team expects to work before they come to the meeting.

LEARNING EXPERIENCE

The facilitation role is about helping the team to not only express their views and opinions, but to also hear and see the alternative perspectives of others. This can be an important learning experience for the team in the early stages of a project as they start to see how their colleagues think and behave in the project environment. Whether they come away from the session with a positive or negative perspective will be heavily influenced by the skills of the facilitator in providing the structure and framework around which the discussion can develop.

Coaching Virtual Teams

Virtual teams face all of the challenges of a team that meets face-to-face, but with a number of significant additional hurdles. I have emphasised the need for the team to build good interpersonal relationships when trying to master complexity. This is much more difficult when the team does not have regular face-to-face contact. Virtual teams are not, therefore, well suited to managing complexity but, as both organisations and projects become increasingly global, there is often no other practical choice.

I would define a virtual project team as a set of individuals assembled to deliver a specific outcome, but who are based in different locations, possibly in different time zones, and whose members may have different cultural backgrounds. The drivers for selecting members who are geographically dispersed may be economic, political or technological.

The critical challenge is to build trust. As described earlier, communication involves a great deal more than writing or talking. Trust comes from picking up the minor signals in our eyes, or our voice or our body language, that indicate sincerity and authenticity. The task of building trust in virtual teams is impeded by the reliance on electronic communication. Poorly considered emails, cultural misunderstandings or simply a perceived lack of response at the other end of the line can all erode whatever trust has been developed at the start of the project.

The style of leadership used in virtual teams is important. A study by Kimberly Furumo and her colleagues (2012) identified that a 'supportive' style of leadership was seen to be more successful than a 'commanding' or directive style as it provides a greater opportunity to develop trust between leader and team member. The style is therefore very much in line with my concept of the PM as leader and coach. Clutterbuck (2007, page 173) considers the challenges of virtual project teams in some depth and points out that 'all of the activities and interventions relevant to coaching the project team apply, but in addition the coach can help the team recognise, understand and manage the more complex communication and motivational issues'.

Peter's Story

We had won a couple of competitions in the UK, pulling virtual teams together to do these BIM challenges where you design and virtually construct a building in 48 hours. We decided to enter an international competition that would require working with a number of teams based in different cities in the UK, Europe and Australia. Based on the lessons learned from the previous events, we worked through all of the issues that we thought could go wrong beforehand. We started looking for other options if the video conferencing equipment stopped working, so we looked at things like Google Hangouts, Face Time, Skype. You can't have the VC running all the time, rooms are booked and so on, so we did make good use of things like one-to-one communication. One of the guys, Mark, spent a lot of time researching the profiles of everybody on the team, so he got all 63 team members to produce a potted bio, like, what is your background, what do you want to get out of this competition, what do you do in your leisure time? Everyone built a nice little CV including a professional photograph and a fun photograph. It worked really well in helping the conversations become more personal. For example someone might say, 'Oh you need to talk to Russell in Brisbane,' or, 'You're the guy who likes windsurfing.' So just by doing that bit of preparation, it allowed us to make human connections.

There are numerous commentators on the challenges and opportunities presented by virtual teams. A search engine enquiry will throw up as much information as you are probably able to absorb on the subject. The common theme running through nearly all of the published material is a need to focus on building personal relationships. From a coaching perspective, the activities and processes required for a virtual project team are not significantly dissimilar from those recommended in this book to deal with face-to-face teams. The difference for a virtual team is that every suggestion that I have included in the book becomes *compulsory*.

Taking the time to set up the team is essential. You need to explore every possible mechanism to improve each member's sense that they have an emotional connection to the men and women at the other end of the line. There is almost total consensus in the literature that you significantly improve your chance of success if you can get everyone together face-to-face, for a couple of days before the project starts. The people-oriented processes and procedures that underpin communication must be co-created and then strictly maintained. Because the forces of dis-engagement are so much stronger for people operating at a distance, the need for one-to-one coaching and mentoring of each team member becomes more critical.

So leading and coaching a virtual project team is, in many ways, far more demanding than running a face-to-face team. The time commitment is much greater, and should not be underestimated. Every relationship needs to be regularly checked, and minor irritations soothed before they become more painful. You also need to periodically introduce new initiatives that keep the team aligned to the project goal and engaged with each other. I believe, however, that if you can successfully coach a virtual team, then you are on your way to mastering the art of team dynamics.

Summary

When the team is immersed in its execution cycle, its performance will reflect the extent to which each member is able to tap into the energy and commitment of the group. This chapter has focused on how you might look at some of the daily interactions so that the team is building trust and reinforcing a sense of having a common goal. Teamwork is an emotional experience, involving a continual cycle of highs and lows. Your role is not necessarily to try and regulate the emotional temperature, as every individual needs to have space to work within the framework of their own personality. It is worth remembering however that people are only human and there will be times when things go wrong, and the collective mood will dip. Every project will have its difficult period. Your objective as leader/coach is simply to try and make sure that the team have more good days than bad ones. This brings us to the question of how to build resilience within the team, which is the subject of the next chapter.

Chapter 6

Building Team Resilience

Layer Four: Building Team Resilience

It is probably not too much of an exaggeration to say that all large projects come under pressure at some stage in their cycle. The implication in the word 'pressure' is that the project team are subjected to competing forces that will push or pull them into actions that were not anticipated at the start of the project. Pressure on the collective group might come from problems such as budget overspend, programme compression or changes in personnel either within the team or in the sponsoring body. As projects and programmes grow in complexity, the likelihood that such pressures will come into play increases. Whether you care to acknowledge it or not, pressure will affect the team's ability to perform. This chapter therefore focuses on the role of leader in coaching the team to develop a sense of resilience.

As part of their research into the field of resilience training, Cary Cooper, Jill Flint-Taylor and Michael Pearn (2013, page 7) pick out five core principles that help inform any discussion on resilience.

1. Individuals vary in both the nature and degree of their ability to cope with pressures and setbacks.

2. Psychological resilience is complex rather than one-dimensional. It is not something that we either have or lack altogether – most of us are resilient in some ways but less so in others.

3. Even the most resilient people have their limits, although they may be less alert to when these limits are being reached.

4. Certain qualities and beliefs, such as optimism or self-confidence, may boost our resilience in most situations but can harm it if they are taken to extremes.

5. Resilience results from the interaction of an individual and the situation.

A team's ability to manage the stresses of change will therefore depend largely on their resilience both as individuals and as a group. Resilience can be defined as the capacity to recover quickly from difficulties. It is recognised as a skill or capability that can be developed. The term is often associated with words like toughness, hardiness and strength. The danger in such terms is that they can perpetuate the idea that stress is a problem that is best ignored, and that all that is required is to muddle through. The stoic philosophy of enduring pain and hardship without showing any emotion is respected in most cultures, right up until someone reaches the point of exhaustion when everything then collapses. Rather than leave the resilience of the team to chance, it is probably a better strategy to put in place whatever provisions you can to enable your team, not only to survive the buffeting winds of change but to actually thrive on the experience.

The words *stress* and *pressure* are often used interchangeably, but in the context of a project it is useful to make a distinction. Stress can be seen as an ongoing state experienced by an individual, usually arising from a mismatch of resources and demands. Pressure is more likely to be episodic, and comes in response to the need to react to specific moments of danger or performance demands. Project teams may experience a collective period of pressure but each member will feel the effects of stress at a different level, according to their particular blend of experience and psychological perspective. So for the purposes of this discussion it is useful to look at pressure in the context of the team, whilst recognising that resilience comes from each individual member's ability to manage the situations that create their particular stressors.

MANAGING STRESS

Put simply, stress is a response to a perception of danger. The danger might be clear and obvious, such as the threat of redundancy or direct personal attack. More often, stress comes from a sense that we can no longer manage to fulfil all of the demands that are being made of us. When we perceive danger, our nervous system starts to produce a number of chemicals. The most notable of these are adrenaline and cortisol, which prepare the body for an immediate response either to freeze, to run or to fight. These chemicals are very useful for managing the direct threat of physical harm. They are, however, potentially damaging to our long-term health when we operate in stressful environments for a prolonged period. In the short term, they also damage our ability to think clearly. Recent advances in neuroscience have allowed researchers to observe how the activity in our brains changes under stressful conditions. In simplistic terms, our emergency response mechanisms push our brains into fast reaction mode, closing down our ability to see the bigger picture. Stressed people therefore become tactical rather than strategic. They can function at an operational level, but left to their own devices will often not make the changes necessary to manage the sources of stress until they reach crisis point.

It is probably not your role to become counsellor/therapist to your team members (although there is no doubt that the process of *really listening* to someone articulate their problems can make a significant improvement in their ability to manage stress). It should however be within your remit to try to regulate the internal team environment. Stressors that commonly come from within the team include:

- a sense of lack of control;
- a sense of a lack of support;
- fear of being excluded;
- fear of intimidation by others;
- loss of security.

If you want your team to perform to the best of its ability then you may need to maintain an overview of the levels of stress being generated within the team. Where it is practical, and within your skill set, you should work to minimise internal stressors. This might involve working with people collectively or on a one-to-one basis. Be careful, however, not to end up increasing your own emotional burden. People under pressure will be stressed as a natural consequence of working on a complex project. Your role is to lead/coach the group so that you can enable them to deliver the outcomes that the project requires. You are not directly responsible for each individual's happiness.

MANAGING PRESSURE

There is a school of thought that a team will perform better if they are kept permanently under pressure. I have heard stories where PMs artificially maintained deadlines and performance goals that were unnecessary. This is a false premise. All of the evidence from research undertaken on stress caused by pressure shows that it has a negative impact on an individual's ability to complete tasks effectively. In the wrong environment, pressure most always damages interpersonal relationships. The studies on people operating in pressurised environments shows that they have a tendency to make more errors of judgement, particularly if unexpected events create a tipping point causing a panic response.

It is possible to see that, in some circumstances, short periods of pressure are good for a team. The need to hit a shared milestone can often be the first test as to whether the group has managed to come together. The interdependencies that are implicit in complex projects start to become much clearer when a deadline is approaching and the team is trying to match resources to task requirements. Pressure can be the catalyst for the emergence of a *real team*. This will only become apparent after the event, as in the heat of the delivery process it is probably quite stressful. Where the dynamics are working well, trust will have developed and each individual will feel a stronger sense of what is possible in the future. The benefits of this new found trust can be compounded if the team is able to recognise and acknowledge the difference. There is potentially a lot of value in taking the time to get the team to do a *learning session* shortly after the first tough deadline has been achieved. Simple questions such as what went well and why? How did you feel before and how do you feel now? These questions allow team members to articulate the positive aspects of the pressure of experience, which helps embed them in the team's mindset. The effect can be to accelerate bonding within the team, making them more resilient for the next challenge.

Hendrie Weisinger and P.T. Pawliw-Fry (2015) have carried out a detailed study of over 12,000 people who were working in high-pressure environments. They then undertook a further investigation of the top 10 per cent of the study group that appeared to be able to continue to work effectively when under pressure. Using a system of 360-degree feedback, they picked out ten of the most common resilient behaviours observed by those who worked with them. These behaviours are summarised below:

1. do not become defensive when criticised;
2. stay calm under pressure;
3. handle setbacks effectively;
4. manage anxiety stress, anger and fear in pursuit of goal;

5. use criticism and other feedback for growth;
6. show a positive outlook;
7. maintain a sense of humour;
8. ability to see things from another's perspective;
9. recognise the effect of their behaviour on others;
10. are able to discuss grievances skilfully.

These are personal qualities, but it is not difficult to see that having people in your team who are able to identify and develop their skill sets in this area will be valuable in helping to pull others through the difficult times. Drawing together their research from a range of different fields, Weisinger and Pawliw-Fry have picked out four key attributes which individuals and teams can work on to develop their resilience. These attributes are set out in Table 6.1.

Table 6.1 Resilience attributes model

Attribute	Features
Confidence	Confidence that your skills and knowledge are sufficient to achieve the desired results increases the ability to work through a period of pressure. Note that there is a danger in being overconfident and missing some important steps. In a team setting, the perception of realistic confidence will impact on the group's collective approach to pressure.
Optimism	Optimism has been shown to have a high correlation with resilience. Optimists will tend to set themselves higher expectations, which are then self-fulfilling. When things go wrong, they are able to create a sense of perspective that puts failure into context and enables them to continue to see a positive future.
Tenacity	Tenacity can be defined as the ability to persevere and sustain the effort towards the long-term goal in spite of setbacks. Studies show that perseverance requires a high degree of focus on clear motivational goals.
Enthusiasm	Having just one member on a team who is able to remain enthusiastic about the future can provide the rest of the team with the energy to remain resilient. Enthusiasm is seen to stimulate positive emotions in ourselves and in others around us, enabling the brain to increase its working memory. This allows us to take in more information and see more potential connections between themes and ideas.

BUILDING RESILIENCE

Taking the above observations into account, what can you do to build resilience in your team? Here are some suggestions.

1. Talk about pressure as part of the team set-up process.
   The purpose is to get your people thinking about a topic that they may never have discussed before. Your role is simply to ask the questions, not necessarily to have the answers. A good starter question is to ask a couple of your more experienced team members how they have managed pressurised situations in the past. Get the team engaged in identifying some potential best practice for managing stress and finding support. Sharing thoughts and feelings has been shown to have a positive and cathartic effect in rebuilding energy and purpose. In a team setting it may take some time for the members to open up and admit to feelings of vulnerability. It becomes easier if the team has gone through some exercises that involved expressing emotions at the start of the project when performance pressure is relatively low.

2. Maintain the sense of control.
   As mentioned above, one of the most common causes of stress is a sense that we have no control over the demands on our resources, and yet we are still held accountable. A useful metaphor is that of an aircraft flying through moderate turbulence. An experienced pilot is aware of what is happening when the plane drops by five metres. For that instant, the plane might be technically out-of-control, yet the pilot knows what is going to happen and so she continues to have a *sense* of control over the aircraft. An inexperienced passenger on the other hand may well be petrified as he has no recognition of the phenomenon and is convinced that the plane is about to fall out of the sky. Other passengers who fly regularly may be more sanguine. They might find the experience uncomfortable but they know that they are probably safe.

   Complex projects are inevitably going to throw up scenarios that are out of your control. A sense of control comes from being able to distinguish between those issues which you can do something about and those which, for the moment at least, are beyond the influence of the team. It is therefore often a matter of maintaining perspective, and dealing with those tasks that are to hand.

3. Be aware of the shift in dynamics when the pressure is on.
Being part of a group stimulates strong emotions that are sometimes consciously, but more often subconsciously, picked up by others in close proximity. These emotions are strong and primitive, being generated by the limbic system that is the part of the brain shared by all mammals. When a group is under pressure the emotional dynamics will become more intense as each member of the team reacts to, and feeds off, the signals coming from the others. This can have both positive and negative consequences. A resilient team will often find their own collective coping mechanisms such as the use of humour to release tension or the use of analysis and reflection.

4. Take the resilience 'temperature'.
When you sense that your team is low on energy, a simple but effective exercise is to start a team meeting by asking the group, 'On the scale of one to ten, how resilient are you feeling at this moment?' By marking the scores on a flipchart or whiteboard you can observe the average 'temperature' of resilience within the team. The next step is to invite each member to elaborate on how they are feeling. I have found this to be a very useful way of getting a team to build empathy and re-engagement. Studies of people under pressure often identify an improvement if they are encouraged to talk about the factors that are creating pressure. Asking the same question at the end of the meeting will often reveal an improvement in the collective rating. The shift is often just a consequence of the collective relaxation that comes from recognising that other teams' members are also feeling the pressure.

5. Take responsibility.
A common trap for many teams under pressure is to begin to see themselves as victims, and seek to blame their situation on others such as the project sponsors, stakeholders or even competing teams. Once you see yourself as a victim, you give up emotional control of the situation. When a team faces setbacks there will inevitably be a need to find a cause. As the group starts to criticise others for their mishaps, it is important to contain the discussion and pull everyone back to the point that the team must take responsibility whatever is happening inside the project. Resilience comes from accepting the situation, agreeing a plan and then taking action.

Coaching the Team to Manage Conflict

Conflict in teams is natural and is not necessarily a bad thing. It would be unusual for a group of individuals who are passionate about a project to be in complete agreement as to how to resolve a problem. Different personality types with different preferences are likely to see an issue from their own perspective and make sense of it through their own psychological filters. Disagreement may even lead to a clash of personalities, and it is easy for dominant personalities to find themselves competing for influence within the team. It is therefore realistic to expect an element of conflict in any project team, particularly when the pressure is on.

The change and uncertainty associated with complexity are likely to create the conditions for disagreement and dispute. The extent to which this damages the team's performance will depend upon how the difference of perspectives is managed, by you as leader and also by the team as a group. A useful starting point is to recognise the distinction between *task-based* conflict and *relationship-based* conflict. Task conflict arises where the dispute is focused on how to resolve a specific problem. *Relationship-based* conflict usually arises from disagreements between team members that are rooted in personal differences.

Clutterbuck (2007) makes the points that whilst *relationship-based conflict* is nearly always damaging to team performance, *task-based conflic*t can be beneficial, particularly when addressing complex problems. In line with many other commentators, he makes the case that having a diversity of views helps the team avoid the tendency towards 'groupthink'. One of the disadvantages of highly cohesive teams is the desire for consensus, which can lead to conformity in the team's thinking process. Crossing the *ingenuity gap* requires creative ideas and the exploration of alternatives. Having people on your team who are prepared to challenge each other's thought process is therefore almost a prerequisite for success. This concept is discussed later in this chapter under the heading of problem solving.

Relationship conflict is a very different problem as it will almost always distract the team from their performance goals. The problem with interpersonal conflict is that the root causes behind it are rarely immediately obvious. It is a fact of life that some people just simply do not get on with each other but cannot explain why that might be. The underlying reasons for our sense of an irrational discomfort with another individual lie in the deeper psychological concepts such as *Projection* and *Transference* which sit outside of the scope of this book. If you want to explore this area in more depth, it is worth reading some of the work by Christine Thornton (2010) who provides a valuable introduction to the psychological processes that are present in most groups.

It is not necessary for everyone on the team to be friends. People can find each other irritating and yet still perform their tasks together quite effectively. If they do not trust each other, however, then their relationship is unlikely to produce the output needed to work in an uncertain project environment. Interpersonal issues are often not immediately obvious. We tend to think of conflict as an aggressive process where two or more parties argue, often with a high degree of emotion. More often, conflict causes the parties to withdraw, and reduce both communication and participation. When open disagreement does surface, it is often over a seemingly minor issue, which suddenly blows up into a heated disagreement that is out of proportion to the matter being discussed.

The coaching challenge is once again to look for the issues that are sitting below the surface. It is about developing an awareness of your subconscious alarm bells that provide an early warning that something is not quite right. Spotting interpersonal differences in the early stages of their development gives you a chance to take action before any major damage is done to the project. There is a judgement call to be made here. When you first spot a potential issue you have to decide whether you should intervene. The temptation is to dismiss your concerns in the hope that individuals will come to their senses. It is more important to find out if there are any underlying trust issues. There are many studies on failed projects where the root cause of breakdown in communication is caused by the perception that one or the other party was not trustworthy.

This is particularly problematic where the team might be made up of subgroups who devolve into factions. Once the subgroup becomes uncomfortable they are inclined to establish a position amongst themselves that becomes reinforced by mutual antipathy. The bedrock of trust upon which any team needs to be built is quickly eroded as the fractions adopt their own, undisclosed position of cautious engagement.

Careful team set-up should have firstly identified any major clashes between individuals or subgroups, and it should also have established a set of behavioural rules that enable conflict to be managed by the team themselves. However, in fast-changing environments there are likely to be times when issues arise which need to be resolved through some form of mediation. When dealing with conflict, team members need to be encouraged to adopt a process of dialogue, where each party approaches the issue with an open mind. The key to resolution by dialogue is allowing the parties to feel that their position is understood. They need to be able to 'talk out the emotion'. The catharsis of being able to explain fears and frustrations out loud often then allows people under stress to relax and become open to the perspectives of others. This creates the opportunity to find common ground and agree a way forward that can keep the project on track.

Problem Solving

Complex problems tend to require creative solutions. Creativity is the use of imagination or original ideas to develop a new approach to an existing problem. The keyword is imagination. This is not necessarily a resource that you can conjure up on demand. People cannot be forced to be imaginative. Indeed, any form of coercion is more likely to diminish creativity than it is to encourage it. The ability to create images and concepts that are novel is a capability that is believed to exist within most human beings. Some people have a natural disposition to spend much of their time exploring new thoughts and ideas, but the capacity to imagine is not restricted to 'right-brained arty types'. As discussed earlier in this chapter, the human brain tends to be most creative when it is not having to manage the chemical and physiological effects of stress.

Nancy Kline (1999) makes a compelling case for recognising that humans will think much more effectively if they are in the right conditions to do so. She emphasises the need to create what she refers to as a 'thinking environment'. This is essentially a meeting between two or more people that is conducted according to set principles and behaviours that will allow each participant to access thoughts and ideas more readily than will occur in the task-focused atmosphere of a typical team meeting. A thinking environment primarily requires giving people the time to think. Logically, a calm environment which feels comfortable and unhurried is going to generate a better response than one that might arise in a rushed meeting with a mixed agenda. Modern life is rarely straightforward but, where you can control the situation, the following factors are likely to generate a better quality of creative output:

1. *The right type of meeting.* Team meetings are probably not the best occasion to tackle complex problems. If the issue is significant then call a separate meeting to allow those attending to really focus on the matter.

2. *The right people.* Having the right people around the table is important. Ideally you need between three and seven contributors. Having a diverse set of backgrounds and opinions will generate a wider range of perspectives.

3. *The right space.* Find a comfortable space in which to meet, away from the interruptions of the team's day-to-day business. It is difficult to think when you're sitting uncomfortably, squeezed around a small table. Having room to move about often helps allow people to stretch and re-energise.

4. *Encourage the use of visual exploration.* Flipcharts, whiteboards and other space to visually map out ideas are also critical. Images and key words allow people to focus and give a platform to develop the streams of thinking. David Seibert (2010) is a strong advocate for the use of wall space to encourage creative thinking. He notes that once people feel that they have enough information, they begin focusing on finding the patterns that will help them make sense of the problem that they are wrestling with. Using visual tools are also a useful way of taking the emotional heat out of a debate. Looking at an image also allows the group to focus on the issue rather than individual.

5. *Think systemically.* Complexity is caused by the interplay of multiple and diverse influences. Problem solving on complex projects will be enhanced if the team can learn to think systemically. As discussed in Chapter 2, systemic thinking is the capacity to look beyond the symptoms of the problem and identify the cause. It can sometimes be helpful to use a systemic model to work through a complex issue. The problem with models is that they work around a process that can sometimes become a means to an end, rather than producing the creative thinking that you need. The text below sets out an example of a problem-solving model based around a series of questions that will prompt the team to take a wider perspective. My recommendation, however, is that you think of it as a checklist rather than a sequential task list.

Systemic Problem Solving Model

Clarity. Is this the real problem? What else lies behind it?

- What are the facts?
- What are my assumptions?
- What emotions may be affecting my judgment?

Understanding. What is going on here?

Desired outcome. What outcome do we now want to achieve?

- What is the best case?
- What is the worst case?

Options.

- What are the extremes that are open to us?
- What are the three best possible solutions

Implications. What is likely to happen? Are there any unintended consequences?

Action. Commit to a plan and execute.

6. *Allow everyone to speak without interruption.* In order to get the most out of a team discussion around the particular issue, Nancy Kline puts a great deal of importance on the need to ensure that each person is allowed to speak without interruption. Her observation is that interruption is highly destructive to our thinking patterns. When someone interrupts us, we often get annoyed and the adrenaline 'kicks in', disrupting the formation of new ideas and connections. She is confident in her assertion that if everyone around the table understands that they will get a turn to speak then, with fewer interruptions, the discussion actually makes faster progress:

> *When people know they will have a turn and be allowed to finish their thought, they think more quickly and say less. When they anticipate interruption, on the other hand, they grasp for the edges of ideas, they rush and they elaborate. Interruption takes up more time than allowing people to sweep cleanly through to the end of an idea (page 109).*

For many teams, this will require breaking the cultural habit where interruption is seen as a mechanism to demonstrate ones intelligence or perspective. As leader/coach you need to help the team learn this new pattern of problem solving and discussion.

Once again, it is easier if this pattern of behaviour is established as part of the ground rules agreed during the set-up process.

7. *Don't search for consensus.* For some teams, particularly those that come from an organisation where consensus is the cultural norm, it can be very difficult to make decisions because the team is not comfortable coming to any conclusion that does not have the positive support of all the members. The paradoxes that result from complexity will often require decisions to be made as a matter of judgement as there will be no clear right or wrong answer. In such circumstances, you may need to help the team to at least recognise the issues from the same perspective, even if they have different opinions on the solution.

Information Search

Finding mechanisms to solve existing problems is therefore an essential skill in any project. As the scale of the programme increases, it is helpful to put in place additional measures that will help the team anticipate problems that may arise in the future. Most of the specialists on resilience advocate the value of trying to avoid unpleasant surprises. When our resources are already overstretched, a new problem coming in from 'left field' can be the factor that leads to the breakdown of the team's ability to function. There are three concepts that can help the early detection of future issues:

1. horizon scanning
2. feedforward
3. feedback.

The remaining part of this chapter looks at each of these concepts in turn.

SCANNING THE HORIZON

Project teams can easily become absorbed in the process of delivery and create their own bubble that isolates them from the realities of the outside world. Complexity on major projects results from a range of variable factors that impose unexpected change. It therefore makes sense to maintain a degree of vigilance on the forces that may create future turbulence. Part of your role as coach/leader is to help the team set up the formal and informal systems to collect data that may have an impact on the project.

At its simplest, this requires little more than establishing protocols which encourage the frequent exchanges of information with a selected number of stakeholders who have a wider field of view than that available to the project team. It is a personal opinion, but I believe that every team should understand, at least at a basic level, the microeconomic factors that drive the commissioning of the project. It is then worthwhile maintaining some sense of what is happening in the outside world that might change these drivers.

More problematic are the uncertainties that are caused by changes in people, and the difficulty in anticipating shifts in behaviours. If, for example, there are political upheavals taking place at the top of the organisation that is sponsoring the project, it might be many months before the ramifications trickle-down to impact on the project. A PM working on a complex transport project told me the following story. The project required a number of external contractors to work side-by-side. The PM noticed that the area director of one of the other external teams had changed. Relationships between the teams had been good up to that point, and the contract had been going reasonably well. He noticed that within a couple of months of the change in leadership, the other team was becoming less collaborative and raising more minor issues that were starting to create tensions which had not been there before. Since the only apparent change was the man at the top, the implication was that he was driving a more transactional approach through his team.

Once again the coaching component of your leadership style needs to think systemically, looking past individual actions to see what is happening in the wider Spheres of Influence. Your horizon-scanning mechanisms should also try to focus on the attitudes and behaviours of those people on the periphery who may be able to influence your project in either a positive or negative way.

Technology offers a variety of options for collecting peripheral data. I have seen a number of phone 'apps' which provide a simple mechanism for requesting and compiling project feedback. Another interesting example is a system called RADAR (http://www.resolex.com/radar.php) which provides a horizon-scanning service designed to identify and manage risk on large projects. Its sophistication is based around a structure which recognises that the information that needs to be passed between informants will change as the project develops. The software is therefore set up to first of all identify any particular risks that arise from the project environment. As the project moves through the cycle, the critical uncertainties change and so enquiries move from a generic focus at the start, to the identification of more specific risks that may be encountered in the later stages of the project.

Such systems are nevertheless no more than tools. Their value depends upon how they are used. Asking people to respond is one thing, but motivating them to provide the requested data is another. In an age when most people struggle to clear their email inbox every day, adding to the burden of activity can lead to a low level of engagement. The key is to find people who care about the project outcome. It is then a matter of nurturing their interest and acknowledging the value of their contribution on a regular basis.

The signs of potential danger need to elicit a balanced response. On the one hand you cannot spend too much time and mental energy worrying about things that may never happen. The more common problem, however, is that many people choose to simply ignore the warning signals until it is too late to take any mitigating action. Risk management processes and procedures are gaining a greater profile as many institutions refocus on governance and risk avoidance. The danger is that too much faith is placed in the process, and not enough on the output that such systems provide. There are many examples of projects that went badly wrong that had immaculately compiled risk registers, but no actions against them. Complexity requires you and your team to make a continuous series of judgement calls. You will not always be right, but with the right early warning systems in place you at least increase your chances of getting lucky.

FEEDFORWARD

Another useful component of your team development strategy is the use of *feedforward* exercises. Feedback is a well-understood mechanism for regulating a system by collecting data which is used to maintain a desired state. Less well understood is the concept of feedforward, where information is collected that is intended to shape the future. The degree of certainty in any project follows a classic S curve, as illustrated in Figure 6.1. In the early stages of any large project there are many questions that still need to be resolved. There is therefore a high level of uncertainty as to how the project will actually play out. As the project progresses, more data is collected and certainty increases to the point that the path to achieving the outcome becomes relatively clear.

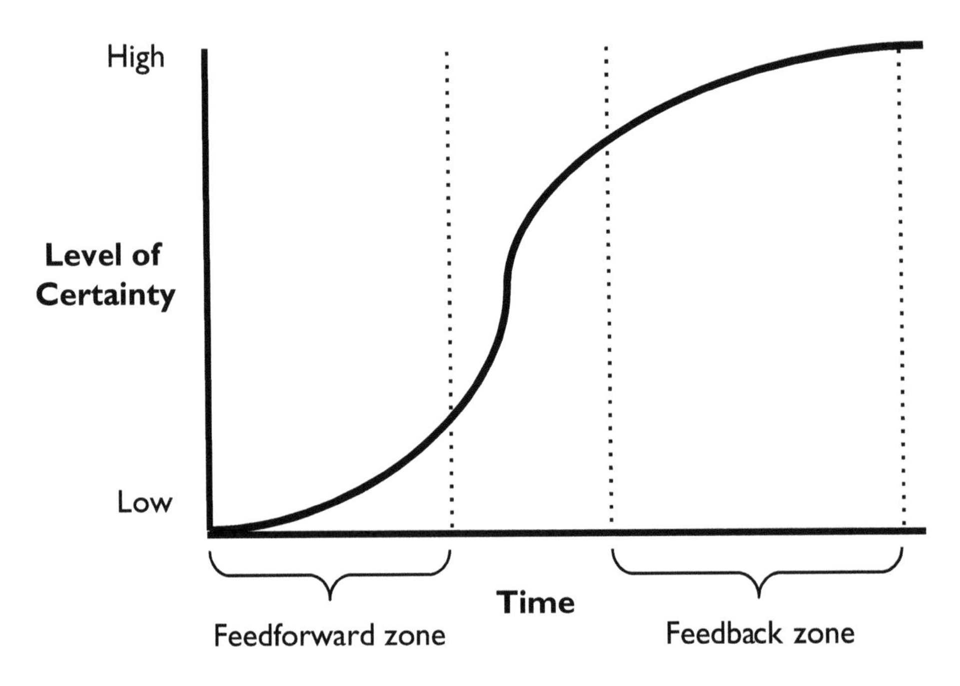

Figure 6.1 Contrasting the phasing of feedforward and feedback

The purpose of a feedforward exercise is to allow the team develop their thinking as to how the project will achieve its objective. Some writers refer to it as a self-fulfilling prophecy, because it helps select a future direction as opposed to accepting the patterns of the past. The most obvious form of feedforward is the creation of the vision that underpins the need for the project. Feedforward becomes a part of the iterative process of working with the project stakeholders to agree what it is that they really want. It is also a useful component of the early agendas of project planning meetings, where the team need to be open to different possible actions that will take the project to the next stage. Feedback systems are designed to collect information to enable one to correct and adjust to a known path. Feedforward, on the other hand, is concerned with looking at the different routes available and deciding which is the most likely to be successful. In some ways feedforward might be seen as another term for scenario planning, and to a certain extent this is true. It depends on the scope of the question. Scenario planning is more often associated with big-picture questions that influence long-term strategy. Feedforward is more project specific.

It is important to recognise the difference between feedforward and problem solving. Feedforward is concerned with helping the team find certainty in the future rather than resolving an issue that has already arisen from the past.

The concept is important because feedforward seeks to obtain inputs from multiple sources, both inside and outside of the project team. Asking stakeholders to provide their thoughts and ideas as to how the project should develop may seem like an admission of a lack of confidence. The actual process is a little more subtle and is tailored to the specific circumstances of a particular project. The objective is to be open to suggestions of alternative strategies and tactics which will help the project's ultimate delivery plan become more certain.

Pre-mortem – A Feedforward Exercise

A good example of feedforward is the idea of undertaking an exercise that could be thought of as a pre-mortem. This is essentially a risk assessment process based around the idea that rather than trying to work out what has gone wrong after the event, you ask your panel of experts (that is, your team) to try and imagine different scenarios that could disrupt the programme.

The idea of a pre-mortem has been around for a while, with a lot of the credit going to Professor Gary Klein (2007). Whilst a pre-mortem could be seen as another form of risk management, there is a key difference. Traditional risk management exercises are a rational process, based on an extrapolation of local sequences of events. A pre-mortem allows the participants to move beyond rational thinking and articulate concerns for which they may have no clear evidence, but are nevertheless potentially very real.

The purpose of the exercise is to use an abstract approach to focus on the future and imagine a scenario where the project has been completed but has not been successful. Each member imagines what might have happened and writes down their different insights on a 'post-it' note. It offers the team members a way of expressing concerns that they would be uncomfortable articulating as a form of criticism. The critical success factor for a pre-mortem is to encourage the group to let go of their particular technical specialisation and to think more broadly.

This is not about finding the wackiest potential risks, but instead using the 'wisdom of crowds'. A variety of studies have shown that collecting answers from a wide variety of people can produce better information than relying solely on the opinions of experts. The beauty of the process is that it engages everyone on the team, and asks them to provide some input in areas *outside* of their professional skill set.

FEEDBACK SYSTEMS TO REGULATE BEHAVIOUR

Internally generated feedback on the team's behaviours will provide you with the best form of data with which to regulate *process loss* within the team. Taking a regular check on the thoughts and feelings of the team as to how they see themselves and others performing allows you to influence any changes that may be necessary to protect the project.

The mechanics for collecting feedback are relatively simple. One just needs to create some type of pro-forma, which can then be circulated, filled in and returned. The level of success that you may have in receiving data that is honest and useful will, however, depend very much on the extent to which the team believe that the output from the feedback is valuable. Teams need to have sufficient trust in the process to feel comfortable providing views and perspectives of themselves and others. In a stressed or transactional team environment, where there are low levels of interpersonal trust, feedback submissions are likely to be guarded as individuals fear the potential for open conflict with others. Alternatively they may fear that such systems will be used to punish them.

Once again, it all depends upon how effectively you are able to establish these behavioural protocols in the set-up phase. The team are more likely to accept the implementation of a feedback system if they feel that they have been party to agreeing its implementation as part of the team's process. Systems that are imposed upon the team are likely to be subverted or ignored, particularly if they are introduced part of the way through the project as a response to project pressure.

Having collected the data, it needs to be fed back to the team so that they can reflect and, when necessary, make adjustments to their behaviour. There may need to be a degree of sensitivity in how this is done. In a calm environment, it is a task that can be carried out by the team leader. There may be times, however, when it is worth considering the use of a neutral third party whose role is specifically to collect and disseminate the feedback.

Mike's Story

Mike relates a great example of the use of feedback within a project team. The project was a Government-funded development of a large scientific facility. The client had recognised early in the project that good team behaviours would be critical to the project's success. He was therefore open to the suggestion from one of his consultants to put in place a system measuring and monitoring various aspects of project performance. The system was built around a set of key performance indicators (KPIs) that included a number of hard and soft measures. It collected the usual KPIs such as cost and programme, but also took a more radical approach by asking for the members' views on the levels of communication, collaboration and also on the stress points within the team. A simple system was set up using an online questionnaire which the team were asked to complete every month.

Information was collected and compiled by one of the consultants. It was then fed back in a one-to-one meeting with each member of the team. Mike recalls that there was a degree of resistance in the early part of the project, particularly from some of the more experienced professionals. The client however took the exercise very seriously and insisted on including himself in the feedback process. This monthly exercise was seen as making a valuable contribution to the development of a highly cohesive team, and was retained in all of the following phases of the development program.

FEEDBACK AND KEY PERFORMANCE INDICATORS

The obsession with control that exists in many hierarchical organisations has seen the proliferation of measurement systems that are designed to try and maintain an element of external control over a project. It is common to find that a team has to regularly submit a set of data that is considered to be its Key Performance Indicators (KPIs). If, as a PM, you know precisely the outcome that your stakeholders are seeking, and you are also clear as to the method of achieving the outcomes, then it is not difficult to set out a number of milestones against which progress can be measured. The problem with KPIs on complex projects is that the boundaries will often keep shifting, so the measures agreed at the start of the project may no longer be the right indicators that the project is on track.

So is team performance about the outcome, or should it be more concerned with how it goes about its work? The answer is invariably both. There is no point in putting in a good team performance without eventually getting the desired results. Every industry has its own set of KPIs, but how should you try and measure ongoing performance in a project environment that keeps changing? Typical KPIs such as time, cost and client satisfaction are still important, at least to the stakeholders, but team performance on complex projects is about trying to assess the factors that affect the 'now', rather than only looking back on measures that show what has happened in the past. It is about how the team:

- find ways of doing things faster;
- find ways of doing things differently;
- finding answers to novel problems;
- find ways to fill in the gaps in competence and capacity within the team.

The team therefore need to find their own measures around team behaviours such as communication, collaboration and participation. These 'soft' skills are difficult to measure empirically but, as I have argued though this book, finding mechanisms that establish and then reinforce collaborative behaviours can have a significant impact on the final outcome. As Clutterbuck (2007, page 79) points out, 'High-performance teams don't waste their time and energy finding solid answers. Instead, they concentrate on making sure that they are asking the right questions, at the right time, so that they can keep abreast of shifting requirements.'

Summary

Managing the team's resilience has not traditionally been seen as an important part of the PM's role. Transactional thinking assumes that everyone should be able to do their job, and if not they can easily be replaced. If someone is struggling that is a personal matter that should not impact on the delivery of the project. I have tried to reinforce the point that as complexity grows it becomes more difficult for *every* member of the team to do their job. How an individual copes with pressure will depend upon what else is going on in the public and private world at any particular moment.

Putting in place processes and activities that can identify and mitigate unnecessary stressors is therefore a type of insurance policy to protect the project. Given the right environment and some encouragement, many teams naturally develop their own support mechanisms. Acts of generosity and kindness stay in the memory for a long time. Finding that your colleagues care enough about you to listen to your problems and to try and provide assistance generates a huge amount of trust and goodwill. This cannot, however, be taken for granted. The culture that the team develops will reflect the attitudes and beliefs of its leaders. When the project first comes under pressure, how you react will be the primary indicator to the team as to the level of support they can be expected to give to the others, and in time, receive themselves.

Chapter 7
So What Have You Learned?

We are approaching the end of this short book on the topic of coaching teams working on complex projects to perform more effectively. So what have you learned? There is more to this question than you might initially imagine. Learning is the acquisition of knowledge or skills through study, experience or being taught. My objective in writing this book was to introduce PMs to the ideas and concepts that explain human behaviour in groups and teams. Reading the texts will have expanded your knowledge, which may be intellectually stimulating but is of little practical value unless you then try something different.

In Part II of the book, I have set out some practical ideas that you might use as the next component of your development of an additional set of skills. The most powerful new learning, however, comes from having your own experiences. Educational experts have concluded that to develop a new skill set you should work to a ratio of 10:20:70, where:

- 10 per cent is knowledge acquired through training or teaching;
- 20 per cent is through expanding your thinking by working with a mentor or coach;
- 70 per cent is through experience and experimentation, practice and reflection.

Learning to Reflect

One of the key components is reflection. At the start of Chapter 4 we discussed the challenges of learning as a team, and the importance of taking time to reflect. The same challenge applies to your personal learning. The process of reflection takes a degree of effort. If your purpose is to really learn from your experience then it helps to think through an event from a systemic outlook.

The ability to pause and mentally critique yourself, not just from your own vantage point, but also taking in the perspective of others, is a useful attribute.

For many people the most difficult part of the reflection process is finding the time to pause. It is one of the bizarre consequences of modern professional life that we seem to have come to a collective conclusion that it is quite logical to take on more commitments in workload then can physically or mentally be accomplished in the time available. As technology has enabled us to work every available hour of the week, we have been lured into a working culture where our commitments to one set of obligations seem to somehow create a secondary set of additional obligations. This is of course just another feature of the complex world in which we now live. If you do not find a way of learning how to manage your commitments however, you may well look back on a life that was unfulfilled. The key is to make space to find *time to think*.

Reflection is a process that can be done by yourself or by working with others. As a solitary exercise, reflection can be quite difficult, primarily because our minds work too quickly to be able to hang onto a single thread of thinking and make sense of it. As soon as one memory comes to mind, a series of additional thoughts immediately distract us from our initial quest. There is a lot to be said for learning to reflect through writing. The art of keeping a journal has become increasingly unfashionable over the years, but those people that do keep a diary maintain that its greatest value is in its therapeutic effect. For technical professionals who are used to writing as a mechanism for passing on information to others, putting pen to paper to create a document that is not intended to be read by anybody else is initially quite a strange experience. I would however urge you to try it. The key is to remember that this is an exercise in *thinking* not communication. The process of writing forces you to slow down and to focus around a particular event or topic. Assembling the words allows you to put your thoughts into order and allows the time to find greater insight to your reaction to your experiences.

Reflection is generally easier when you can work with somebody else. An experienced coach will have the skills to draw out a stream of consciousness and to challenge you to think at a deeper level. If the resources are not available to use an external coach then it is worth exploring the idea of *co-coaching*. It is sometimes enough simply to be able to talk to someone knowing that they will not interrupt you. Finding a like-minded colleague who also understands the power of listening will enable you to coach each other. If you're not sure where to start with this process go back and look at the pages on asking Questions and Listening in Chapter 2.

Belief is Critical to Success

Earlier in this book I talked about developing your team coaching practice into a philosophy as to how you work as a PM. If you come into the PM role from a technical perspective, this is not always an easy progression. In the course of my research for this book, I asked an experienced consultant whether he considered that the team coaching role could be filled by a PM? He thought for a minute before replying and then commented, 'Yes, it might be possible, but only if the PM really believed in what he/she was doing.' This is a significant insight. Whilst you may grasp the logic of the need to manage a complex project in a different way, to adopt a people-centric or coaching style effectively, you need to believe that it works.

It's not just what you do, but how you do it, that is going to make the difference. The techniques and process described in the earlier chapters are a familiar component of many team development courses. The critical factor that makes the difference as to whether an action will have an impact or not is the conviction with which the process is applied. A philosophy could be described as a set of guiding principles that support your thought process for making decisions. I see the development of a working philosophy as a continual work-in-progress. A paradigm shift might help you look at an old problem in a new light, but a working philosophy informs every aspect of your role. Transactional philosophies are fairly simple in that they are typically short term and numerical. Building a collaborative philosophy is more complex and I suggest that you should accept that it will take some time to develop. As you explore and experiment you will find those techniques and practices that work well and those that are less effective. As you gain confidence so you will also gain belief.

Maturity in Complexity

Throughout this book I have tried to emphasise that managing complexity requires a different approach to that offered by the traditional project management methodologies. Learning to come to terms with continual change and uncertainty is a state of mind that also develops overtime. As discussed in earlier sections, human beings have an amazing capacity to adapt to difficult situations, but to do so requires making the necessary mental adjustments. Peter Robertson (2005, page 74) uses the phrase 'maturity in complexity', which he describes as 'the ability to respect complexity, not to avoid paradoxes, to accept dilemmas, and not to fall back on simplification by seeing every event as part of a cause-and-effect cycle'. He points out that maturity in complexity is not the same as experience, in that someone can have plenty of experience but still continue to make the same mistakes.

My perception is that one of the keys to developing your maturity in complexity is to be able to flip from your engagement at the project 'coalface' to the bird's eye view that comes from taking a systemic perspective. Maturity is a positive word. It is not tied to age but instead implies that you have reached a level of expertise where your judgement is now able to take in a wider set of variables. Learning to quickly analyse a situation from the different Spheres of Influence will in time become a valuable leadership habit. This is tied to the ability to question yourself and others in a spirit of genuine enquiry that will enable you to seek deeper explanations as to how you might address the root cause of a problem, not just its symptoms.

A Skill Set for the Future

I have also argued that when the forces that create change become difficult to predict, you need to rely more heavily on the problem-solving capacity of human beings who are personally committed to the success of your project. I believe quite passionately that learning to think, and helping others to think, is a critical skill for survival and success in the twenty-first-century. I do not see this skill set as optional.

Looking into the future, it is possible to envisage a world where the majority of projects must be delivered within a complex environment. There is a growing consensus that the old hierarchical management models used by so many large organisations are becoming obsolete. The argument, elegantly put forward by Frederick Laloux (2014), is that in a complex world, any attempt to accurately forecast events, even in the short term, is increasingly futile. As organisations have grown, they have become stuck with the challenge that they cannot make decisions upon anything that cannot either be proven or observed. Reporting hierarchies require recommendations to be presented in papers and slide decks. Numbers have become the primary basis for the decision to 'turn left or right'.

Laloux's argument is that most large organisations have become embedded in a management mindset that could be described as *predict and control*. This requires senior managers to anticipate the future and guess the revenues and associated costs for the period ahead. Systems are then put in place to attempt to control the workforce to deliver the 'guesses'. It is not difficult, however, to see how the forces of multiplicity, interdependence and diversity will quickly destroy any predictive models, putting stress on the system. The stresses are primarily borne by those people working in the organisation, trying to bend the reality of day-to-day activity to fit into a forecast of the future that was out of date shortly after it was committed to paper.

Vlatac Hlupic (2014) sites a litany of statistics that indicate that the current management model used in large organisations is in decline. She points to surveys showing that only 20 per cent of employees say they feel fully engaged at work, and that only one in ten believe that they have a future career with their current employer. Such statistics also reflect declining performance, with return on assets (ROA) dropping progressively since 1965 and the decreasing life expectancy of large companies. The average lifespan of a Fortune 500 company has now fallen from 75 to 15 years over the last 50-year period. Hlupic observes:

> *Business as usual will not work any more. Instead of just focusing on numbers, processes and structures, management needs to focus on people, their values, the ability of a person to make a positive difference, trust, higher purpose, integrity, loyalty, compassion, the need for togetherness and to be part of something bigger than themselves. Businesses have to view people as sources not as resources (page 20).*

The management and organisational shifts that writers such as Laloux and Hlupic anticipate cannot happen without more people learning, practising and advocating the skills of human engagement that have been set out in this book. The practices such as articulating a *compulsive vision, building resilience* and *really listening* are just as valid when working with a standing group as they are for a project team.

The underlying theme of this book has been to encourage a shift of mindset, from a *command and control* style that emanates from the transactional paradigm to a different type of leadership which acknowledges that, in the modern world, no one person can know all the answers. The skill set that I have advocated is focused on working with teams to find creative responses to novel problems. I believe that the key to managing complexity is to facilitate the connections that people make with each other to obtain the full set of potential information available, so that human ingenuity can be used to find the best course of action. The traits that the modern world needs more than ever before are those that help humans manage their fears and find the confidence to explore.

The shift to a collaborative style of leadership requires some level of intrinsic motivation. Without a personal sense of wanting to achieve something more than making money, I think that it is difficult to genuinely move beyond the transactional mindset. So my final question is, what motivates you once your material needs have been satisfied? Do you know the path that will help you feel satisfied and fulfilled in your career and your life? For all of the problems created by our complex world, I see that there are more opportunities to shape our own future than were available to past generations.

As a PM you have the skills that the world needs. It is often seen as a rather trite aspiration to want to make the world a better place, but if you can manage complex projects successfully, you have a genuine opportunity to do just that. There are many people who would like to do more to make a difference to our planet, but lack a clear sense of how. A good start would be to teach them how to coach a team.

References

Bass, B.M. (1990) *Bass & Stogdill's Handbook of Leadership Theory, Research and Managerial Applications*, 3rd ed. Free Press, New York.

Cavanagh, M. (2012) *Second Order Project Management*. Gower, Farnham.

Clutterbuck, D. (2007) *Coaching the Team at Work*. Nicholas Brealey, London.

Cooper, C., Flint-Taylor, J. and Pearn, M. (2013) *Building Resilience for Success: A Resource for Managers and Organisations*. Palgrave Macmillan, London.

Covey, S.R. (1992) *The Seven Habits of Highly Effective People: Powerful Lessons in Personal Change*. Simon and Schuster, London.

Covey, S.M.R. (2006) *The Speed Of Trust: The One Thing That Changes Everything*. Simon and Schuster, New York.

Earley, C. and Mosakowski, E. (2000) 'Creating hybrid team cultures: An empirical test of transnational team functioning'. *The Academy of Management Journal*, Vol. 43, No. 1, pp. 26–49.

Furumo, K., De Pillis, E. and Buxton, M. (2012) The Impact of Leadership on Participation and Trust in Virtual Teams, SIGMIS-CPR 2012, Proceedings 50th Annual Conference, ACM, New York.

Gersick, C. (1988) 'Time and transition in work teams: Toward a model of group development'. *Academy of Management Journal*, Vol. 31, No. 1, pp. 9–42.

Gratton, L. and Erickson, T.J. (2007) 'Eight ways to build collaborative teams'. *Harvard Business Review*, November 2007.

Hackman, J.R. and Wageman, R. (2005) 'A Theory of Team Coaching'. *Academy of Management Review*, Vol. 30, No. 2, pp. 269–87.

Hancock, D. (2010) *Tame, Messy and Wicked Risk Leadership*. Gower, Farnham.

Hawkins, P (2011) *Leadership Team Coaching*. Kogan Page, London.

Homer-Dixon, T. (2000) *The Ingenuity Gap: Facing the Economic, Environmental, and Other Challenges of an Increasingly Complex and Unpredictable Future*. Knopf, New York.

Hills, J., Norton, L. and North, S. (2014) *Brain-Savvy Leading: Neuroscience, Tips and Tools*. Head Heart + Brain, London.

Hlupic, V. (2014) *The Management Shift: How to Harness the Power of People and Transform Your Organisation for Sustainable Success*. Palgrave Macmillan, London.

Hofstede, G., Hofsted, J.H. and Minkov, M. (2010) *Cultures and Organisations, Software of the Mind: Intercultural Cooperation and Its Importance for Survival*. McGraw Hill, New York.

Honey, P. and Mumford, A. (1992) *The Manual of Learning Styles*. Peter Honey Publications, London.

Kahneman, D. (2011) *Thinking, Fast and Slow*. Penguin, London.

Kantor, D. (2012) *Reading The Room: Group Dynamics for Coaches and Leaders*. John Wiley and Sons, San Francisco.

Karlsen, W. and Wheeler, A. (2014) http://www.thefairlightproject.com/five-spheres-influence, accessed 30 April 2015.

Katzenback, J. and Smith, D. (1993) *The Wisdom of Teams: Creating the High-Performance Organisation*. Harper Business Essentials, New York.

Klein, G. (2007) 'Performing a project premortem'. *Harvard Business Review*, September 2007.

Kline, N. (1999) *Time to Think: Listening to Ignite the Human Mind*. Cassell Illustrated, London.

Kolb, D. (1984) *Experiential Learning: Experience as the Source of Learning and Development*. Prentice-Hall, New Jersey.

Laloux, F. (2014) *Reinventing Organisations: A Guide to Creating Organisations Inspired by the Next Stage of Human Consciousness*. Nelson Parker, Belgium.

Lencioni, P. (2002) *Death by Meeting. A Leadership Fable.* Jossey Bass, San Francisco.

McGregor, D. (1960) *The Human Side of Enterprise*. McGraw Hill, New York.

McQuire, J.B. and Tang, V. (2011) 'Slow Down to Speed Up', Forbes Online, www.forbes.com/2011/02/23/slow-down-speed-efficiency-leadership-managing-ccl.html, accessed 5 March 2015.

Myers, I.B. (1998) *Introduction to Type*, 6th Ed. CPP Inc, Sunnyvale, CA.

Porter, E. (1976) 'On the development of relationship awareness theory: A personal note'. *Group & Organization Management*, September, No. 1, pp. 302–9.

Quinn, R.E. (1988) *Beyond Rational Management: Mastering the Paradoxes and Competing Demands of High Performance*. Jossey-Bass, San Francisco, CA.

Robertson, P. (2005) *Always Change a Winning Team: Why Reinvention and Change are Pre-requisites for Business Success*, Marshall Cavendish, Singapore.

Royal Institution of Chartered Surveyors (2014) *Stakeholder Engagement*, 1st ed, www.rics.org.

Royal Institution of Chartered Surveyors (2015) *Construction Pathway Guide – Project Management*, www.rics.org.

Sargut, G. and McGrath, R.G. (2009) 'Learning to live with complexity'. *Harvard Business Review*, September 2009.

Schein, E. (2010) *Organisational Culture and Leadership*, 4th ed. Jossey Bass, San Francisco, CA.

Schein, E. (2013) *Humble Enquiry: The Gentle Art of Asking Instead Telling*. Berret-Koehler, San Francisco, CA.

Schutz, W. (1958) *FIRO: A Three-dimensional Theory of Interpersonal Behaviour*. Will Shutz Associates, London.

Schwarz, R. (2002) *The Skilled Facilitator*. Jossey-Bass, San Francisco, CA.

Seibert, D. (2010) *Visual Meetings: How Graphics, Sticky Notes and Idea Mapping Can Transform Group Productivity*. John Wiley & Sons, Hoboken, NJ.

Senge, P. (2006) *The Fifth Discipline, The Art and Practice of the Learning Organisation*. Random House, London.

Skiffington, S. and Zeus, P. (2000) *The Complete Guide to Coaching at Work*. McGraw-Hill, New York.

Son, J. and Rojas, E.M. (2011) 'Impact of optimism bias regarding organizational dynamics on project planning and control'. *Journal of Construction Engineering and Management*, Vol. 137, No. 2, pp. 147–57.

Thornton, C. (2010) *Group and Team Coaching*. Routledge, Hove, UK.

Tuckman, B. (1965) 'Developmental sequence in small groups'. *Psychological Bulletin*, Vol. 63, No. 6, pp. 384–99.

Tyssen, A.K, Wald, A. and Speith, P. (2013) 'The challenge of transactional and transformational leadership in projects'. *International Journal of Project Management*, Vol. 32, No. 3, pp. 365–75.

Weisinger, H. and Pawliw-Fry, J.P. (2015) *How to Perform Under Pressure: The Science of Doing Your Best When it Matters Most*. John Murrey Learning, London.

Whitmore, J. (2003) *Coaching for Performance: Growing People, Performance and Purpose*, 4th Ed. Nicholas Brearley Publishing, London.

Yukl, G.A. (2001) *Leadership in Organizations*, 5th ed. Prentice Hall, Upper Saddle River, NJ.

Zeus, P. and Skiffington, S (2000) *The Complete Guide to Coaching at Work*. McGraw Hill, Sydney.

Index

Page numbers in **bold** refer to figures and tables.

Advances in Project Management

Advances in Project Management provides short, state of play, guides to the main aspects of the new emerging applications including: maturity models, agile projects, extreme projects, Six Sigma and projects, human factors and leadership in projects, project governance, value management, virtual teams and project benefits.

Currently Published Titles

Advances in Project Management, edited by Darren Dalcher
978-1-4724-2912-4

Project Ethics, Haukur Ingi Jonasson and Helgi Thor Ingason
978-1-4094-1096-6

Managing Project Uncertainty, David Cleden 978-0-566-08840-7

Managing Project Supply Chains, Ron Basu 978-1-4094-2515-1

Project-Oriented Leadership, Ralf Müller and J. Rodney Turner
978-0-566-08923-7

Strategic Project Risk Appraisal and Management, Elaine Harris
978-0-566-08848-3

The Spirit of Project Management, Judi Neal and Alan Harpham
978-1-4094-0959-5

Sustainability in Project Management, Gilbert Silvius, Jasper van den Brink, Ron Schipper, Adri Köhler and Julia Planko 978-1-4094-3169-5

Second Order Project Management, Michael Cavanagh 978-1-4094-1094-2

Tame, Messy and Wicked Risk Leadership, David Hancock 978-0-566-09242-8

Managing Quality in Projects, Ron Basu 978-1-4094-4092-5

Managing the Urgent and Unexpected, Stephen Wearne and Keith White-Hunt 978-1-4724-4250-5

A Practical Guide to Dealing with Difficult Stakeholders, Jake Holloway, David Bryde and Roger Joby 978-1-4094-0737-9

Customer-Centric Project Management, Elizabeth Harrin and Phil Peplow 978-1-4094-4312-4

Reviews of the Series

PROJECT ETHICS, HAUKUR INGI JONASSON AND HELGI THOR INGASON

> *This book will instil more confidence in the PM profession and will help individuals become better practitioners.*
>
> *PM World Journal*, vol. II, no. V

> *Project leaders managing any type of project but especially large complex projects with a diverse stakeholder group would benefit from this book. By adding the ethical analysis to the risk assessment management plan, the project leader will consider the broader implication of the project.*
>
> *PM World Journal*, vol. III, no. VII

MANAGING PROJECT UNCERTAINTY, DAVID CLEDEN

> *This is a must-read book for anyone involved in project management. The author's carefully crafted work meets all my '4Cs' review criteria. The book is clear, cogent, concise and complete…it is a brave author who essays to write about managing project uncertainty in a text extending to only 117 pages (soft-cover version). In my opinion, David Cleden succeeds brilliantly…For project managers this book, far from

being a short-lived stress anodyne, will provide a confidence-boosting tonic. Project uncertainty? Bring it on, I say!

International Journal of Managing Projects in Business

Uncertainty is an inevitable aspect of most projects, but even the most proficient project manager struggles to successfully contain it. Many projects overrun and consume more funds than were originally budgeted, often leading to unplanned expense and outright programme failure. David examines how uncertainty occurs and provides management strategies that the user can put to immediate use on their own project work. He also provides a series of pre-emptive uncertainty and risk avoidance strategies that should be the cornerstone of any planning exercise for all personnel involved in project work.

I have been delivering both large and small projects and programmes in the public and private sector since 1989. I wish this book had been available when I began my career in project work. I strongly commend this book to all project professionals.

Lee Hendricks, Sales and Marketing Director, SunGard Public Sector

The book under review is an excellent presentation of a comprehensive set of explorations about uncertainty (its recognition) in the context of projects. It does a good job of all along reinforcing the difference between risk (known unknowns) management and managing uncertainty (unknown unknowns – 'bolt from the blue'). The author lucidly presents a variety of frameworks/models so that the reader easily grasps the varied forms in which uncertainty presents itself in the context of projects.

VISION – The Journal of Business Perspective (India)

Cleden will leave you with a sound understanding about the traits, tendencies, timing and tenacity of uncertainty in projects. He is also adept at identifying certain methods that try to contain the uncertainty, and why some prove more successful than others. Those who expect risk management to be the be-all, end-all for uncertainty solutions will be in for a rude awakening.

Brad Egeland, *Project Management Tips*

PROJECT-ORIENTED LEADERSHIP, RODNEY TURNER AND RALF MÜLLER

Müller and Turner have compiled a terrific 'ready-reckoner' that all project managers would benefit from reading and reflecting upon to challenge their performance. The authors have condensed considerable

experience and research from a wide variety of professional disciplines, to provide a robust digest that highlights the significance of leadership capabilities for effective delivery of project outcomes. One of the big advantages of this book is the richness of the content and the natural flow of their argument throughout such a short book...Good advice, well explained and backed up with a body of evidence...I will be recommending the book to colleagues who are in project leader and manager roles and to students who are considering these as part of their development or career path.

Arthur Shelley, RMIT University, Melbourne, Australia,
International Journal of Managing Projects in Business

In a remarkably succinct 89 pages, Müller and Turner review an astonishing depth of evidence, supported by their own (published) research which challenges many of the commonly held assumptions not only about project management, but about what makes for successful leaders.

This book is clearly written more for the project-manager type personality than for the natural leader. Concision, evidence and analysis are the main characteristics of the writing style...it is massively authoritative, and so carefully written that a couple of hours spent in its 89 pages may pay huge dividends compared to the more expansive, easy reading style of other management books.

Mike Turner, Director of Communications for NHS Warwickshire

STRATEGIC PROJECT RISK APPRAISAL AND MANAGEMENT, ELAINE HARRIS

...Elaine Harris's volume is timely. In a world of books by 'instant experts' it's pleasing to read something by someone who clearly knows their onions, and has a passion for the subject...In summary, this is a thorough and engaging book.

Chris Morgan, Head of Business Assurance
for Select Plant Hire, Quality World

As soon as I met Elaine I realised that we both shared a passion to better understand the inherent risk in any project, be that capital investment, expansion capital or expansion of assets. What is seldom analysed are the components of knowledge necessary to make a good judgement, the impact of our own prejudices in relation to projects or for that matter the cultural elements within an organisation which impact upon the decision making process. Elaine created a system to break this down and give reasons and logic to both the process and the human interaction necessary

to improve the chances of success. Adopting her recommendations will improve teamwork and outcomes for your company.
Edward Roderick Hon LLD, Former CEO Christian Salvesen Plc

TAME, MESSY AND WICKED RISK LEADERSHIP, DAVID HANCOCK

This book takes project risk management firmly onto a higher and wider plane. We thought we knew what project risk management was and what it could do. David Hancock shows us a great deal more of both. David Hancock has probably read more about risk management than almost anybody else, he has almost certainly thought about it as much as anybody else and he has quite certainly learnt from doing it on very difficult projects as much as anybody else. His book draws fully on all three components. For a book which tackles a complex subject with breadth, insight and novelty – its remarkable that it is also a really good read. I could go on!

Dr Martin Barnes CBE FREng, President,
The Association for Project Management

This compact and thought provoking description of risk management will be useful to anybody with responsibilities for projects, programmes or businesses. It hits the nail on the head in so many ways, for example by pointing out that risk management can easily drift into a check-list mindset, driven by the production of registers of numerous occurrences characterised by the Risk = Probablity × Consequence equation. David Hancock points out that real life is much more complicated, with the heart of the problem lying in people, so that real life resembles poker rather than roulette. He also points out that while the important thing is to solve the right problem, many real life issues cannot be readily described in a definitive statement of the problem. There are often interrelated individual problems with surrounding social issues and he describes these real life situations as 'Wicked Messes'. Unusual terminology, but definitely worth the read, as much for the overall problem description as for the recommended strategies for getting to grips with real life risk management. I have no hesitation in recommending this book.

Sir Robert Walmsley KCB FREng, Chairman of the
Board of the Major Projects Association

In highlighting the complexity of many of today's problems and defining them as tame, messy or wicked, David Hancock brings a new perspective to the risk issues that we currently face. He challenges risk managers, and particularly those involved in project risk management, to take a much broader approach to the assessment of risk and consider the social, political and behavioural dimensions of each problem, as well as the scientific and engineering aspects with which they are most comfortable. In this way, risks will be viewed more holistically and managed more effectively than at present.

Dr Lynn T. Drennan, Chief Executive, Alarm,
the Public Risk Management Association

SUSTAINABILITY IN PROJECT MANAGEMENT, GILBERT SILVIUS, JASPER VAN DEN BRINK, RON SCHIPPER, ADRI KÖHLER AND JULIA PLANKO

Sustainability in Project Management thinking and techniques is still in its relatively early days. By the end of this decade it will probably be universal, ubiquitous, fully integrated and expected. This book will be a most valuable guide on this journey for all those interested in the future of projects and how they are managed in a world in peril.

Tom Taylor dashdot and vice-President of APM

Project Managers are faced with lots of intersections. The intersection of projects and risk, projects and people, projects and constraints... Sustainability in Projects and Project Management is a compelling, in-depth treatment of a most important intersection: the intersection of project management and sustainability. With detailed background building to practical checklists and a call to action, this book is a must-read for anyone interested in truly implementing sustainability, project manager or not.

Rich Maltzman, PMP, Co-Founder, EarthPM, LLC, and co-author of
Green Project Management, Cleland Literature Award Winner of 2011

Great book! Based on a thorough review on existing relevant models and concepts the authors provide guidance for different stakeholders such as Project Managers and Project Office Managers to consider sustainability principles on projects. The book gets you started on sustainability in project context!

Martina Huemann, WU-Vienna University of Economics
and Business, Vienna Austria

While sustainability and green business have been around a while, this book is truly a 'call to action' to help the project manager, or for that matter, anyone, seize the day and understand sustainability from a project perspective. This book gives real and practical suggestions as to how to fill the sustainability/project gap within your organization. I particularly liked the relationship between sustainability and 'professionalism and ethics', a connection that needs to be kept in the forefront.

David Shirley, PMP, Co-Founder, EarthPM, LLC, and co-author of *Green Project Management,* Cleland Literature Award Winner of 2011

It is high time that quality corporate citizenship takes its place outside the corporate board room. This excellent work, which places the effort needed to secure sustainability for everything we do right where the rubber hits the road – our projects – has been long overdue. Thank you Gilbert, Jasper, Ron, Adri and Julia for doing just that! I salute you.

Jaycee Krüger, member of ISO/TC258 a technical committee for the creation of standards in Project, Program and Portfolio Management, and chair of SABS/TC258, the South African mirror committee of ISO/TC258

Sustainability is no passing fad. It is the moral obligation that we all face in ensuring the future of human generations to come. The need to show stewardship and act as sustainability change agents has never been greater. As project managers we are at the forefront of influencing the direction of our projects and our organisations. Sustainability in Project Management offers illuminating insights into the concept of sustainability and its application to project management. It is a must read for any modern project manager.

Dr Neveen Moussa, Project Manager, Adjunct Professor of Project Management and past president of the Australian Institute of Project Management

About the Series Editor

Professor Darren Dalcher is founder and Director of the National Centre for Project Management, a Professor of Project Management at the University of Hertfordshire and Visiting Professor of Computer Science at the University of Iceland.

Following industrial and consultancy experience in managing IT projects, Professor Dalcher gained his PhD from King's College, University of London. In 1992, he founded and chaired of the Forensics Working Group of the IEEE

Technical Committee on the Engineering of Computer-Based Systems, an international group of academic and industrial participants formed to share information and develop expertise in project and system failure and recovery.

He is active in numerous international committees, standards bodies, steering groups, and editorial boards. He is heavily involved in organising international conferences, and has delivered many international keynote addresses and tutorials. He has written over 150 refereed papers and book chapters on project management and software engineering. He is Editor-in-Chief of the *International Journal of Software Maintenance and Evolution*, and of the *Journal of Software: Evolution and Process*. He is the editor of a major new book series, Advances in Project Management, published by Gower Publishing which synthesises leading edge knowledge, skills, insights and reflections in project and programme management and of a new companion series, Fundamentals of Project Management, which provides the essential grounding in key areas of project management.

He has built a reputation as leader and innovator in the area of practice-based education and reflection in project management and has worked with many major industrial, commercial and charitable organisations and government bodies. In 2008 he was named by the Association for Project Management as one of the top 10 influential experts in project management and has also been voted *Project Magazine's* Academic of the Year for his contribution in 'integrating and weaving academic work with practice'. He has been chairman of the APM Project Management Conference since 2009, setting consecutive attendance records and bringing together the most influential speakers.

He received international recognition in 2009 with appointment as a member of the PMForum International Academic Advisory Council, which features leading academics from some of the world's top universities and academic institutions. The Council showcases accomplished researchers, influential educators shaping the next generation of project managers and recognised authorities on modern project management. In October 2011 he was awarded a prestigious Honorary Fellowship from the Association for Project Management for outstanding contribution to project management.

He has delivered lectures and courses in many international institutions, including King's College London, Cranfield Business School, ESC Lille, Iceland University, University of Southern Denmark, and George Washington University. His research interests include project success and failure; maturity and capability; ethics; process improvement; agile project management; systems and software engineering; project benchmarking; risk management; decision making; chaos and complexity; project leadership; change management; knowledge management; evidence-based and reflective practice.

Professor Dalcher is an Honorary Fellow of the Association for Project Management, a Chartered Fellow of the British Computer Society, a Fellow of the Chartered Management Institute, and the Royal Society of Arts, and a Member of the Project Management Institute, the Academy of Management, the Institute for Electrical and Electronics Engineers, and the Association for Computing Machinery. He is a Chartered IT Practitioner. He is a Member of the PMI Advisory Board responsible for the prestigious David I. Cleland Project Management Award; of the APM Group Ethics and Standards Governance Board, and, until recently; of the APM Professional Development Board. He is a member of the OGC's International Reference Group for Managing Successful Programmes; and Academic and Editorial Advisory Council Member for *PM World Journal,* for which he also writes a regular column featuring advances in research and practice in project management.

National Centre for Project Management
University of Hertfordshire
MacLaurin Building
4 Bishops Square
Hatfield, Herts, AL10 9NE
Email: ncpm@herts.ac.uk

For Product Safety Concerns and Information please contact our EU representative GPSR@taylorandfrancis.com
Taylor & Francis Verlag GmbH, Kaufingerstraße 24, 80331 München, Germany

www.ingramcontent.com/pod-product-compliance
Ingram Content Group UK Ltd.
Pitfield, Milton Keynes, MK11 3LW, UK
UKHW051831180425
457613UK00022B/1204
* 9 7 8 0 3 6 7 7 3 7 5 8 0 *